Pressure Sensitive
Popular Musicians under Stress

Geoff Wills and Cary L. Cooper

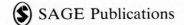 SAGE Publications

London · Newbury Park · Beverly Hills · New Delhi

© Geoff Wills and Cary L. Cooper 1988

First published 1988

SAGE Publications Ltd
28 Banner Street
London EC1Y 8QE

SAGE Publications India Pvt Ltd
C-236 Defence Colony
New Delhi 110 024

SAGE Publications Inc
2111 West Hillcrest Street
Newbury Park, California 91320

SAGE Publications Inc
275 South Beverly Drive
Beverly Hills, California 90212

British Library Cataloguing in Publication Data

Wills, Geoff
    Pressure sensitive : popular musicians
    under stress.——(Sage communications in
    society).
    1. Popular music. Musicians. Stress
    I. Title II. Cooper, Cary L. (Cary Lynn),
    1940–
    780'.42'019

    ISBN 0–8039–8141–4
    ISBN 0–8039–8142–2 Pbk

Library of Congress catalog card number 88–060145

Printed in Great Britain by J.W. Arrowsmith Ltd, Bristol

Contents

Foreword
by Rick Wakeman

We have all heard of Keith Moon, Jimi Hendrix, Janis Joplin, Elvis Presley, John Bonham of Led Zeppelin, Paul Kossoff of Free, and Phil Lynott, to name but a few of the famous musicians who have died in recent years.

If the list were to include the not-so-famous, it would fill this book.

I'm sure that 'drug overdose' or 'heart failure due to a mixture of drink and drugs' are satisfactory answers for the tabloids, and probably suit their needs, but undoubtedly the real causes lie much deeper.

Popular musicians are not special people, but they are unique, in as much as they are placed in a position of power and wealth, very quickly, and usually for a very short period of time. When the bubble bursts, the trappings of success still live within, now heavily bandaged with the realities of life.

I can say categorically that the average person could not cope with this, and here is the root of the problem. Musicians are just average people. A simple musical gift places them upon the fragile pedestal.

Sadly, all this tends to happen at a young age, which makes it extremely difficult to cope with.

Contrary to popular opinion, musicians are not all 'thick' either. For my own part I have 'O' levels and 'A' levels, and a college education to boot, but I still managed to drink to such excess that I became one of the 'unwilling alcoholics' and smoked to such an excess that I spent weeks in hospital following heart problems. These excesses were caused in part by marriage breakups, financial traumas, the death of my father, and the fact that nobody ever really understands what makes a musician tick.

I'm still here. Older, wiser, teetotal, and a non-smoking golfer!

Why, God only knows. I don't deserve to be, and that's why this survey fascinated me. It started to make me realize that stress is not just for the middle-aged businessman, but very much for the young unsuspecting musician.

What good can come of the findings in this book, I don't know, but at least there is now an awareness.

Dead musicians can't make music. I hope we can keep music live.

Acknowledgements

We are indebted to all the popular musicians who took part in this study, giving their valuable time to questionnaires and interviews. We would also like to thank the British Musicians' Union for their support.

Grateful acknowledgment is made to the following for permission to reprint previously published material:

Excerpts from *Making Music* edited by George Martin. Copyright 1983. Used with permission of Pan Books Ltd and William Morrow.

Excerpts from *Stormy Weather* by Linda Dahl. Copyright 1984. Used with permission of Quartet Books Ltd and Pantheon Books.

Excerpt from *Stress and Music* edited by M. Piparek. Copyright 1981. Used with permission of Wilhelm Braumüller, Universitäts-Verlagsbuchhandlung GmbH.

Excerpt from *Expensive Habits* by Simon Garfield. Copyright 1986. Used with permission of Faber and Faber Ltd and A.D. Peters and Co. Ltd.

Excerpt from *The Who: Maximum R & B* by Richard Barnes. Copyright 1982. Used with permission of Richard Barnes, Pete Townshend and Eel Pie Publishing Ltd.

Excerpt from *The Playboy Interview: Allen Klein*. November 1971, page 92. Copyright © 1971. Used with permission of Playboy Magazine.

Excerpts from *The Jazz Life* by Nat Hentoff, published by Da Capo Press Inc. Copyright © 1977 by Nat Hentoff. Used with permission of International Creative Management Inc.

Excerpt from 'dBs can be Hazardous to your Health' by Martin Polon, *Recording Engineer/Producer*, October 1979. Copyright © 1987 Intertec Publishing Corporation. Used with permission of Intertec Publishing Corporation, Overland Park, Kansas.

1
Stress at work: an overview

It has become a truism to say that stress in everyday life is greater than it has ever been. In recent years, research has focused especially on occupational stress, and studies have been carried out, for instance, on the police (Davidson and Veno, 1980), teachers (Kyriacou, 1980), dentists (Cooper, 1980c), tax officers (Cooper and Roden, 1985), and executives (Marshall and Cooper, 1979). A relatively neglected area for research, however, has been that relating to the stresses involved in working in the popular arts, even though these arts make a large and important contribution to society. In covering one area of the popular arts, the aim of the present volume is to redress the balance to some extent. But before

Table 1.1 *Mortality due to ischaemic heart disease among males 1968–1977 (40–69 age group)*

Rank order	Country	Deaths (per 100,000)
1	Finland	673
2	Scotland	615
3	Northern Ireland	614
6	USA	528
7	Ireland	508
8	England & Wales	498
	West Germany	325
	Bulgaria	237
	Poland	229
	France	152
	Japan	69

Country	Decrease (%)	Country	Increase (%)
USA	−27	Scotland	+1
Japan	−25	England & Wales	+3
Austria	−20	Northern Ireland	+12
Finland	−18	Ireland	+30
Norway	−11	Hungary	
Holland	−10	Poland	
Italy	−2	Rumania	over 30
		Bulgaria	
		Yugoslavia	

Source: WHO 1982

moving on to our study of popular musicians, it is helpful to set it in context against the larger background of occupational stress as a whole.

Stress-related illnesses such as alcoholism, coronary artery disease and mental ill health are costing British industry a fortune. The Centre for Health Economics estimates that over £1.3 billion alone is lost each year due to alcoholism in industry (£641.51 m as a result of sickness absence, £567.70 m due to premature death, etc.) The World Health Organization has published figures which indicate that not only is the United Kingdom near the top of the world league table in terms of mortality due to heart disease, but also is showing substantial yearly increases, while many other countries are showing declines for the first time this century – particularly those countries where industry has introduced health promotion and stress management programmes for its employees. But why is the UK so far behind? Can we begin to identify the sources of occupational stress, and what can we do about them? What role can psychologists play in reversing the rising trend of occupational ill health?

Table 1.2   *Mortality due to ischaemic heart disease among females 1968–1977 (40–69 age group)*

Rank order	Country	Deaths (per 100,000)
1	Scotland	202
2	Israel	193
3	Northern Ireland	189
5	USA	171
6	Ireland	168
9	Finland	142
10	England & Wales	138
	Bulgaria	110
	West Germany	84
	Italy	63
	France	37
	Japan	29

Country	Decrease (%)	Country	Increase (%)
Japan	−39	Scotland	+10
USA	−31	England & Wales	+11
Italy	−20	Hungary	
Finland	−15	Poland	
France	−14	Rumania	over 20
Norway	−2	Bulgaria	
Northern Ireland	0	Yugoslavia	

Source: WHO 1982

The costs of stress

Let's start at the beginning. Why is it that many countries (for example, US, Finland) seem to be showing declines in their levels of stress-related illnesses (for example, heart disease, alcoholism), while those in the UK are still rising? Is it the case, for example, that American employers are becoming more altruistic and caring for their employees, and less concerned about simply making a profit? Two trends in the US are forcing American firms to take action. First, American industry is facing an enormous and ever-spiralling bill for employee health care costs. Individual insurance costs rose by 50 per cent over the past two decades, but the employers' contribution rose over 140 per cent. It has also been estimated that over $700 million a year is spent by American employers to replace the 200,000 men aged 45 to 65 who die or are incapacitated by coronary artery disease alone. Top management at Xerox estimate that losing just one executive to a stress-related illness costs the organization $600,000. In the UK, however, employers can allow intolerable levels of stress on their employees, and it's the taxpayer who picks up the bill, through the National Health Service. There is no direct accountability or incentive for firms to maintain the health of their employees. Of course, the indirect costs are enormous, but rarely does the firm actually attempt to estimate this cost; they treat absenteeism, labour turnover and even low productivity as an intrinsic part of running a business.

Secondly, there is another source of growing costs, too. More and more employees, in American companies at least, are litigating against their employers, through the worker compensation regulations and laws, in respect of job-related stress. For example, in California, the stress-related compensation claims for psychiatric injury now total over 3,000 a year since the California Supreme Court upheld its first stress-disability case in the early 1970s. The California labour code now states specifically that workers' compensation is allowable for disability or illness caused by 'repetitive mentally or physically traumatic activities extending over a period of time, the combined effect of which causes any disability or need for medical treatment'. California may be first; but what happens there has a habit of reaching other places after a longer or shorter time-lapse.

In the UK, we are just beginning to see a move towards greater litigation by workers about their conditions of work. Several unions are supporting cases by individual workers, and the trend is certainly in the direction of future disability claims and general damages being awarded on the basis of 'cumulative trauma' in the UK.

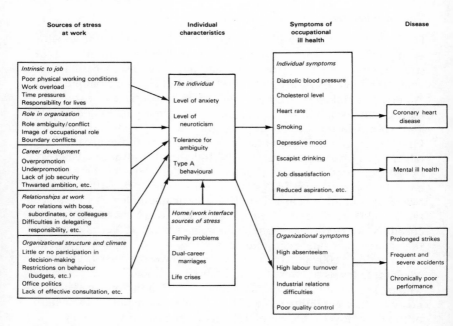

Figure 1.1 *A model of stress at work*

The sources of stress

In order for something to be done about the consequences of stress in the workplace, we have to understand the sources of stress (see Figure 1.1).

Factors intrinsic to the job
Sources of stress intrinsic to the job across a variety of occupations include poor physical working conditions, shift work, work overload or underload, physical danger, person–environment fit (P–E) and job satisfaction (Cooper and Smith, 1985).

Poor physical working conditions Poor physical working conditions can exacerbate stress at work. In regard to nuclear power plant operators, for example, Otway and Misenta (1980) believe that the design of the control room itself is an important variable in terms of worker stress. They propose that control room designs need to be updated, requiring more sophisticated ergonomic designs. Furthermore, they refer to a study which highlighted an important stress factor in the Three Mile Island accident as being the distraction caused by excessive emergency alarms.

In a study carried out by Kelly and Cooper (1981) on the stressors associated with casting in a steel manufacturing plant, they found poor physical working conditions to be a major stressor. Many of the stressors were concentrated in the physical aspects of noise, fumes, and to a lesser extent, heat, plus the social and psychological consequences of isolation and interpersonal tension.

Shift work Numerous occupational studies have found that shift work is a common occupational stressor. It affects neurophysiological rhythms, such as blood temperature, metabolic rate, blood sugar levels, mental efficiency, and work motivation, which may ultimately result in stress-related disease (Monk and Tepas, 1985). A study by Cobb and Rose (1973) on air traffic controllers found four times the prevalence of hypertension, and also more mild diabetes and peptic ulcers, among the subjects than in their control group of second class airmen. Although these authors identified other job stressors as being instrumental in the causation of these stress-related maladies, shift work was isolated as a major problem area.

Job overload French and Caplan (1972) see work overload as being either quantitative (having too much to do) or qualitative (being too difficult), and certain behavioural malfunctions have been associated with job overload (Cooper and Marshall, 1980). For example, in a study of air traffic controllers, Crump et al. (1981) found that one of the primary short-term but uncontrollable stressors was 'being overloaded'. They devised a unique method of measuring job stress, using the repertory grid technique, which allowed them to assess the sources of stress among air traffic controllers in terms of a number of paired constructs (for example, controllable/uncontrollable and long-term/short-term stress).

In another investigation of stress among British police officers, Cooper et al. (1982) found that work overload was a major stressor among the lower ranks, particularly police sergeants. In particular, sergeants who scored high on the depression scale of the Middlesex Hospital Questionnaire tended to be older operational officers who believed they were overloaded, and who perceived a number of bureaucratic and outside obstacles to effective police functioning. They complained about the long hours and heavy work load, as well as the increased paperwork, lack of resources and the failure of the courts to prosecute offenders.

Job underload Job underload associated with repetitive, routine, boring and understimulating work has been associated with ill health (Cooper and Smith, 1985). Moreover, in certain jobs, such as airline pilots, air traffic control etc., periods of boredom have to be accepted, along with the possibility that one's duties may suddenly be disrupted due to an emergency situation. This can give a sudden jolt to the physical and mental state of the employee and have a subsequent detrimental effect on health. Furthermore, boredom and lack of interest in the job may reduce the individual response to emergency situations.

Physical danger   There are certain occupations which have been isolated as being high risk in terms of potential danger, for example, police, mine workers, airline pilots, soldiers and firemen. However, stress induced by the uncertainty of physically dangerous events is often substantially relieved if the employee feels adequately trained and equipped to cope with emergency situations.

Role at work

A person's role at work has been isolated as a main source of occupational stress, involving role ambiguity (that is, conflicting job demands), responsibility for people and conflicts stemming from organizational boundaries.

After reviewing the relevant literature, Kasl (1973) concluded that correlations between role conflict and ambiguity, and components of job satisfaction, tend to be strong (on the other hand, correlations with mental health measures tend to be weak). However, personality differences are important determinants in how an individual reacts to role conflict, and greater job-related tension is produced in introverts than in extroverts. French and Caplan (1972) also hold that flexible people show greater job-related tension under conditions of conflict than do rigid individuals.

Degree of responsibility for people and their safety also appears to be a potentially significant occupational stressor. Kroes (1976), for example, sees responsibility for people as a potential stressor for police, although not to the extent that it is for air traffic controllers. This has recently been verified by a study of occupational stress in air traffic controllers, which isolated responsibility for people's safety and lives as a major long-term occupational stressor (Crump et al., 1981).

The problems that role conflicts can generate were amply demonstrated by Cooper et al. (1978) in their investigation into dentists. It was found that the variables which predicted abnormally high blood pressure among dentists were factors related to the role of the dentist, that is, that he considers himself to be 'an inflictor of pain' rather than 'healer'; that he has to carry out non-clinical tasks such as administrative duties, sustaining and building a practice; and his role also interferes with his personal life, primarily in terms of time commitments.

Career development
The next group of environmental stressors is related to career development, which Cooper (1983) has found to be a fundamental stressor at work, and refers to 'the impact of overpromotion, underpromotion, status incongruence, lack of job security, thwarted ambition'. Status congruency or degree to which there is job advancement (including pay grade advancement) was found by Erickson et al. (1972) in their large sample of Navy employees, to be positively related to military effectiveness and negatively related to the incidence of psychiatric disorders.

Career development blockages are most notable among women managers, as a study by Davidson and Cooper (1983) revealed. In this investigation, the authors collected data from over 700 female managers and 250 managers at all levels of the organizational hierarchy and from among several hundred companies. It was found that women suffered significantly more than men on a range of organizational stressors, but the most damaging to their health and job satisfaction were the ones associated with career development and allied stressors (for example, sex discrimination in promotion, inadequate training, male colleagues treated more favourably, not enough delegation to women).

Relationships at work
Relationships at work, which include the nature of relationships and social support from one's colleagues, boss and subordinates, have also been related to job stress. According to French and Caplan (1972), poor relationships with other members of an organization may be precipitated by role ambiguity in the organization, which in turn may produce psychological strain in the form of low job satisfaction. Moreover, Caplan et al. (1975) found that strong social support from peers relieved job strain and also served to condition the effects of job stress on cortisone levels, blood pressure, glucose levels and the number of cigarettes smoked (as well as cessation of cigarette smoking).

In addition, where male executives had problems, they were associated with problems in relationships, as Cooper and Melhuish (1980) discovered in their study of 196 very senior male executives. It was found that male executives' predispositions (for example, outgoing, tough-minded, etc.) and their relationships at work were central to their increased risk of high blood pressure. They were particularly vulnerable to the stresses of poor relationships with subordinates and colleagues, lack of personal support at home and work, and to the conflicts between their own values and those of the organization.

Organizational structure and climate

Another potential source of occupational stress is related to organizational structure and climate, which includes such factors as office politics, lack of effective consultation, lack of participation in the decision-making process and restrictions on behaviour. Margolis et al. (1974) and French and Caplan (1972) found that greater participation led to higher productivity, improved performance, lower staff turnover and lower levels of physical and mental illness (including such stress-related behaviours as escapist drinking and heavy smoking).

Home/work pressures

A danger of the current economic situation is the effect that work pressures (such as fear of job loss, blocked ambition, work overload and so on) have on the families of employees. At the very best of times, young managers, for example, face the inevitable conflict between organizational and family demands during the early build-up of their careers (British Institute of Management, 1974). But during a crisis of the sort we are currently experiencing, the problems increase in geometrical proportions as individuals strive to cope with some of their basic economic and security needs. As Pahl and Pahl (1971) suggest, most individuals under normal circumstances find home a refuge from the competitive and demanding environment of work, a place where they can get support and comfort. However, when there is a career crisis (or stress from job insecurity as many employees are now facing), the tensions the individuals bring with them into the family affect the spouse and home environment in a way that may not meet their 'sanctuary' expectations. It may be very difficult, for example, for the spouse who is beginning to feel insecure and worried about the family's economic, educational and social future, to provide the kind of supportive domestic scene the partner requires.

It is against this background of occupational stress and its possible alleviation, therefore, that we now move on to the subject of this book: the popular musician.

2

Who are popular musicians, and where are they coming from?

Eric (not his real name) is aged 34. He is an eminent rock musician, who has worked in recording sessions, as a member of famous bands, and as a bandleader in his own right. At one time he consumed eighty cigarettes and two bottles of Scotch per day, and suffered three heart attacks, cirrhosis of the liver, and two broken marriages. He now has his health problems under control, but he recalls vividly the stresses he encountered in charge of a rock band touring America:

> You get up in the morning, and the hotel's lost your clothes, you've had no sleep because there was a late interview the night before, the car to take you to the airport hasn't shown up, so you've got to try and get a taxi. The plane's delayed an hour and a half, you take off, it's a lousy flight, bouncing all over the place. When you get to the soundcheck at the gig, you find the gear hasn't arrived because the truck's got a puncture, and it's an important gig because that's the one that all the Press are going to be at. So you go to your hotel and think 'I'd really like a drink.' You go to the bar, and somebody comes up to you who obviously likes all your records and says, 'Hey do you like it here?' You feel like turning round and saying, 'Why don't you —— off and get out of my sight?' But that person goes away, and tells millions of people what a nasty, horrible person you are, so you have to say, 'Everything's great'. You can't tell them your problems because they go round saying, 'Hey, they're having terrible problems, and we'll be lucky if there's a show tonight.' So you feel like a Jekyll and Hyde. Then you go on stage, and find half your gear's not working, so you bull —— your way through the gig – that's a frightener. You've come 5,000 miles, it may only be a little backwater city in America, but they only see you once every two years. And you get very stroppy with people. It's very hard.

Eric was one of the musicians interviewed in the investigation into stress in popular musicians. He is lucky, in that he is still alive. At the time of writing, the deaths of two eminent rock musicians have recently been reported in the press: one due to a fatal car accident, the other as a result of heroin addiction. Indeed, the regular reporting in the popular press of the premature deaths or arrests for drug abuse of musicians is just one indication that the professional musician who works in the field of popular music, which encompasses jazz and jazz-influenced music, rock, pop and 'commercial' music, appears to be particularly subject to stress. And yet the popular musician is a member of an occupational group that has been virtually ignored in the academic literature. This is surprising since he plays such a large part in the public consciousness and in the media. It may be that he is seen to be involved in a somewhat trivial pursuit, not worthy of serious study, when compared with colleagues who play classical music, and about whom there are a number of studies with regard to the effects of stress. However, one needs only to look at figures for the sales of records as just one pointer to the impact that the popular musician makes on the public. This is illustrated in Table 2.1. In record sales alone, the popular musician is involved in making a large contribution to the national income.

Table 2.1   *World sales of popular records in millions, 1980*

Country	Singles	LPs	Cassettes
USA	157	308	184
Canada	17	54	16
Argentina	7	7	7
Europe	259	372	133
USSR	–	204	–
Japan	75	120	80
Australia	11	21	14
South Africa	7	5	4

Source: Wright (1983)

Of course, the making of records is only one of the activities that the popular musician may indulge in. It is helpful here to define what is meant by the term 'popular musician' with regard to this book. The popular musician is a musician who earns his living by playing music which falls outside the context of symphonic or classical music. In the context of the study which forms the basis of this book, only the British popular musician is referred to, although his counterpart in other countries is probably very similar in terms of his activities and the stresses from which he suffers.

Although popular music has a somewhat amorphous quality, and is sometimes difficult to fit into categories, it falls into three main areas. These are: rock and pop; jazz; and commercial music. Rock and pop is the type of music which forms the content of programmes on the BBC's Radio One. Jazz, in all its forms, whether traditional, mainstream, modern, or avant garde, is the music originated by Black American musicians. Commercial music is the type of music which forms a large part of the content of programmes on the BBC's

Radio 2. It derives to a great extent from the music of dance bands and theatre shows of the 1920s, 1930s and 1940s.

The popular musician works in a number of settings. These may be live engagements, or 'gigs', in musicians' parlance, and can take place in such diverse situations as stadia, theatres, concert halls, ballrooms, cabaret clubs, jazz clubs, and on ocean-going liners, or they may be recording sessions which occur in record, television and radio studios.

It is difficult to state how many professional popular musicians there are at the present time. However, the British Musicians' Union currently has 40,000 members, and more than half of these work in the popular field (Evans, personal communication, 1983). Though newspaper reports frequently provide evidence of the stresses to which eminent rock stars are subjected, 'there has been little systematic study of . . . the everyday working musician', to quote Davies (1978).

Since this book is based on a study of British professional popular musicians, it may be helpful to sketch in a brief history of popular music in Britain as a background.

After the First World War, an era commenced which lasted for two decades. This has been referred to as the 'Golden Age of the Dance Bands' (see, for instance, Godbolt, 1984). A craze for dancing to American music swept the country, and hotels, restaurants, nightclubs and the local Palais de Danse employed dance bands. A list of bandleaders who achieved fame and fortune, wearing their frock-coats and waving their batons, would include Bert Ambrose, Jack Hylton, Jack Payne, Billy Cotton, Henry Hall, Roy Fox, Lew Stone and Debroy Somers. As well as working in 'live' situations, dance band musicians began to make records and radio broadcasts. As Ehrlich (1985) states, broadcasts began in 1923, and by 1926 more than two million licence-holders were able to listen to the London Radio Dance Band twice a week. By 1927, a weekly BBC schedule contained 16 per cent of dance music. In 1928, Jack Payne became director of the BBC Dance Orchestra. By 1939, the number of radio licences held by members of the public had increased to nine million and, due to revenue from licence fees, the BBC became one of the largest employers of musicians.

The dance bands contained many musicians whose first love was jazz, but who had to play commercial music to make a living. Although it was impossible to survive playing jazz live at this time, a number of dance bands, including those of Bert Ambrose, Lew Stone and Jack Hylton, made records which often had a high jazz content. A core of musicians, including trumpeter Tommy McQuater, trombonist George Chisolm, saxophonists Buddy

Featherstonhaugh, Billy Amstell, Freddy Gardner, Danny Polo and Sid Phillips, drummer Max Bacon and guitarist Ivor Mairants, played on these recordings.

After the Second World War, things were never the same for the dance bands. A number of the more accomplished dance band musicians including Billy Amstell (see Amstell, 1986) moved into radio and TV sessions as the number of arrangers and musical directors, such as Stanley Black, Bob Sharples, Peter Knight and Eric Robinson, proliferated.

The period from 1945 to 1955 represented the heyday for large touring dance bands based on the American model. These bands, such as those of Ted Heath, provided employment for musicians who would later make their mark as jazz or session musicians, and also placed emphasis on featured vocalists such as Dickie Valentine.

In the 1940s, two separate jazz movements rose to prominence, namely revivalist jazz and modern jazz. Revivalist or traditional jazz was sparked by the emergence of George Webb's Dixielanders, and paved the way for the 'trad' boom of the 1950s and early 1960s, bringing acclaim to bands such as those led by Acker Bilk, Chris Barber and Kenny Ball. British modern jazz was spearheaded by a group of young musicians, largely Jewish, who had gained their grounding in dance bands and had heard the original modern jazz in New York on their visits when playing in bands on transatlantic liners. Among their number were Ronnie Scott, Tony Crombie, Tommy Pollard and Laurie Morgan.

In the mid 1950s British popular music was taken in a new direction with the advent of rock and roll. A group of singers, of whom the first was Tommy Steele, emerged, imitating their American counterparts. Initially they were accompanied by dis-gruntled modern jazz musicians, but soon a group of young musicians who played only rock, and who were based around the Two I's coffee bar in Soho, arrived. The prototypical rock musicians of this era, highly influential and extremely accomplished in their own style, were Cliff Richard's backing group the Shadows. The three guitar and drums line-up utilized by the Shadows formed the basis for much of the popular music created in the next decade with the advent of Mersey Beat and the pop group boom of the early and mid 1960s. Rock music threw up its own virtuoso instrumentalists, who owed nothing to the previous dance band or jazz eras, for instance, musicians such as the guitarists Jimi Hendrix, Eric Clapton and Jeff Beck.

Thus, a series of often confusingly diverse strains came to make up the fabric of popular music. The past twenty years has seen the development of the rock and pop music business into a worldwide, multimillion pound industry. Few popular musicians, even those who have not actively sought contact with it, have avoided its influence.

Today, a large proportion of popular musicians still play only pop and rock, but in the late 1960s the barriers began to break down between rock and jazz, and a form of music known as jazz–rock became popular. The mainstay of popular music is still perhaps the freelance musician, and in the past number of years a new breed has emerged. Though still with his roots in the dance band tradition, unlike the purely rock musician, he is a more versatile creature who can turn his hand to both rock and jazz with equal aplomb (see, for instance, Coryell and Friedman, 1978). He often takes as his inspiration the eminent American recording session players such as David Sanborn, Mike Brecker and Steve Gadd, who play what is known as 'fusion' music. This, then, is the backdrop against which today's popular musician plays, whether he is involved in jazz, rock, or any of the music in between.

It was as a result of conversations with musicians on the topic of stress that the idea for the current book arose. Common themes which emerged included the pressures of travelling, loss of sleep, pressures on personal relationships, lack of job security and the constant pressure to produce something creative or commercially acceptable. There is a certain resentment towards the general public, who often voice the opinion that the musician 'is paid a lot of money for doing something he enjoys – he ought to get a real job'. Relating to this, a recent record by the group Dire Straits, entitled 'Money for Nothing', ironically describes this view.

It appears that the popular musician is involved in a difficult, worthwhile and often lonely profession, bringing pleasure to the public, and money to the country. The authors decided that this was an area which required further investigation in order that the pressures, problems and stress outcomes were recognized and tackled. Clearly, there was a need for detailed research, in order to isolate more precisely the specific stresses being experienced by professional popular musicians, and the subsequent detrimental stress outcomes.

3
Musicians under stress: a review of the literature

The stress model

The research described in this book is based upon the multifaceted model of occupational stress proposed by Cooper and Marshall (1976), and updated by Davidson and Cooper (1981). This model not only acknowledges the importance of occupational sources of stress, but also brings into focus factors extraneous to the specific work situation, namely what have been termed extra-organizational factors. The two main extra-organizational areas which have been pinpointed as sources of stress are (1) personality and individual differences, and (2) the home environment, encompassing marital and financial concerns. In taking all these factors into account, the reciprocal effects of stressors in the work, home and social environments are acknowledged.

Following the framework laid down by Davidson and Cooper, the model is adapted for the purposes of this book by looking at the following factors which are relevant to occupational stress in professional popular musicians:

1 Personality

2 The home environment

3 Occupational sources of stress
  (a) Factors intrinsic to the job
    (i) Performance anxiety
    (ii) Physical stress
    (iii) Physical danger
    (iv) Poor physical work conditions
    (v) Shift work
    (vi) Work overload
    (vii) Person–environment fit and job satisfaction
  (b) Career development
  (c) Relationships at work
  (d) Organizational structure and climate

4 Stress outcomes
  (a) Occupational stressors and physical illness

(b) Occupational stressors and psychological health
(c) Alcoholism
(d) Drug abuse

When an individual experiences stress, from either an occupational or an extra-organizational source, this will manifest itself in a stress outcome, or outcomes, specific to that individual. This is obviously an 'individual within context' situation, so that when one individual is exposed to a stressor he may become involved in drug abuse, while another may engage in excessive drinking.

In reviewing the literature regarding stress and popular musicians, we encounter certain problems, since there has been a lack of academic attention to this topic. In an intensive search of the literature, the authors were able to trace only one academic study of occupational stress and professional popular musicians. However, there does exist a fairly extensive literature on certain aspects of stress and its effects on classical musicians, and since many of the problems that the classical musician encounters are parallel to those of the popular musician, it is highly relevant to review this literature in the present context.

In the absence of academic studies of the popular musician, there nevertheless exists a huge, and ever-growing, popular literature on all aspects of popular music, often in the form of biographies and accounts of different aspects of the popular music business. It was felt, therefore, that it was appropriate to draw from these popular sources to illustrate aspects of both occupational and extra-organizational stressors where academic material was lacking.

In looking at the literature relating to musicians, certain factors stand out as having special relevance to this occupational group. With regard to extra-organizational factors, the role of personality is given special emphasis. If it is accepted that the musician is a member of a 'creative' profession, he must be viewed in the context of studies of the creative personality. Research has pointed to links between creativity and psychological disturbance, and from this point of view, the musician may be an individual especially susceptible to stress.

Turning to potential stressors in the work environment, particular attention is given to the effects of performance anxiety. This is a factor of special importance to musicians, and indeed to members of the performing arts as a whole, but it is one which has not been previously covered in the occupational stress literature.

Recent research (for example, Cooper and Davidson, 1982) has focused on the effects of occupational stress on women. In the light of this research, therefore, the effects of stress on women musicians are reviewed.

Finally, with regard to potentially detrimental stress-induced outcomes, the question of drug abuse is focused upon, since it is a topic which excites great interest in the media and among members of the public.

The creative personality and psychological disturbance

Numerous studies of the creative personality in many fields of endeavour have been carried out, and a link has frequently been observed between creativity and emotional instability. In the light of these studies, as someone involved in creative work, the musician may be a person particularly prone to stress.

The work of the Institute of Personality Assessment and Research at Berkeley, under the direction of Mackinnon (1962), was concerned with creativity in architects, writers and mathematicians. Using the Minnesota Multiphasic Personality Inventory, it was consistently shown that creative subjects showed greater psychopathology than did controls on the scales measuring depression, hypochondriasis, hysteria, psychopathy and paranoia.

Cross et al. (1967), using the Sixteen Personality Factor Questionnaire in a study of the personalities of practising artists and writers, found that their subjects scored high on the factors I (tender-minded and sensitive) and Q4 (tense and overwrought). Csikszentmihalyi and Getzels (1973) carried out a study of 94 male advanced art students, also using the 16PF. It was found that, compared to other college males, the artists scored significantly higher on the factors C (emotionally less stable), H (timid), I (tender-minded), O (apprehensive), and Q4 (tense).

Further studies, by Gotz and Gotz (1979a,b), utilized the Eysenck Personality Questionnaire. This was administered to 147 male professional artists living in West Germany, and it was found that the artists scored significantly higher than controls on the dimensions of introversion, neuroticism and psychoticism.

Personality studies of musicians

Prior to the present study, no academic personality studies exist of popular musicians. However, there are a number of studies of the personalities of classical musicians, and there is evidence to suggest that there are links with the personality characteristics of other creative individuals, not least in the area of emotional instability.

Trethowan (1977) carried out a study of eminent composers. He examined the lives of 60 subjects, all deceased, and selected them because relevant information about them was readily available. Bearing this bias in mind, it was found that the subjects exhibited between them virtually the whole range of identifiable psychiatric illness or personality disorders. The commonest and most important of these were clinically recognizable affective disorders, and half the subjects, including Elgar, Peter Warlock, Beethoven, Robert Schumann, Balakirev, Rossini and Holst, fell in this category. In sharp contrast, it was only possible to identify one composer, Ivor Gurney, who suffered from a schizophrenic illness. Almost as many composers exhibited neurotic or abnormal personality traits. One subject, Johann Strauss, suffered severely from phobic anxiety, while a number of others had obsessional personalities; these included Bruckner, Lully, Mahler, Ravel, Satie, Scriabin, Chopin and Dvořák. Those who appeared to have had some other form of personality disorder included Beethoven, Berlioz, Busoni, Gluck, Liszt, Paganini, Pfitzner, Tchaikovsky and Wagner. Four of the subjects committed suicide. It must be remembered, of course, that composers represent only one sub-section of musicians as a whole. Moreover, these were eminent musicians, and therefore may not be representative of more rank-and-file performing musicians.

Kemp (1981) studied the personalities of a large sample of both student and professional musicians, using the 16PF. The sample of student musicians contained 688 subjects aged between 18 and 25, and they were found to differ significantly from controls on introversion, as measured by factors A (reserved), F (sober), and Q2 (self-sufficient); and on anxiety, as measured by factors C (emotionally less stable), O (apprehensive) and Q4 (tense). The sample of professional musicians contained 202 subjects aged between 24 and 70, and for this group strikingly similar results were obtained. They also differed significantly from controls on introversion, as measured by factors A (reserved) and Q2 (self-sufficient); and on anxiety as measured by factors C (emotionally less stable), L (suspicious), O (apprehensive), and Q3 (undisciplined self-conflict). Thus, there is evidence that musicians show traits of introversion and anxiety at an early stage in their development, and these traits remain present in their professional lives.

In looking at the question of whether different instrumentalists have different personality characteristics, Kemp (1980) studied 625 music students aged between 18 and 25, again using the 16PF. It was found that brass players were significantly more extroverted than other instrumentalists, as measured by factors F (happy-go-lucky) and Q2 (group-dependent), and also less sensitive, as measured by factor I (tough-minded). These findings are similar to those of Davies (1978), who interviewed members of a Glasgow-based symphony orchestra, using the Eysenck Personality Inventory. Davies found that brass players were highest on extroversion and lowest on neuroticism, while string players were highest on neuroticism. In terms of which instrumentalists are likely to succumb to stress due to their personality characteristics, it appears, therefore, that brass players are the least at risk.

Further evidence of emotional instability in musicians comes from a survey by Piparek (1981), who studied 24 members of the Vienna Symphony Orchestra, using interview data and unspecified projection and association tests. The author found that neuroticism scores were 5 per cent higher in musicians than those of other professions which he had studied.

Thus, in summing up, it can be stated that, from the evidence of personality studies, musicians overall show a tendency to be somewhat introverted and anxious, not unlike their colleagues in other creative fields. These traits may make them especially open to the effects of stress.

The home environment

In looking at the way that home and family life can be disrupted as a result of occupational stressors, it is necessary to consider the fact that stressors at work can also affect both family and social life. The professional musician works mainly in the evening, and is often away from home on tour. In addition, work may come in at short notice, thus disrupting further any home or social life. When not working, the dedicated musician will be involved in practice or rehearsal, and this can lead to jealousy on the part of spouses who often feel rationed in terms of time allocation with their partners. An additional underlying fear harboured by the spouses of musicians is that, while on tour, the musician will fall prey to the charms of the 'groupie' (see Herman, 1982).

In a study of the effects of stress on members of the Vienna Symphony Orchestra, Schulz (1981) asked 107 musicians to rate what they considered to be high stressors. 33 per cent stated that they had to take holidays at an unfavourable time of year, 21 per cent stated that they did not have enough leisure time, while 13 per cent felt that their work caused undue interference with their family life. Raeburn (1984), in a study of occupational stress in professional rock musicians, found that a conflict between career and other social roles was one of the most frequently and intensively experienced stressors.

It has been found that the family life cycle is a U-shaped curve with a decline in satisfaction over the earlier stages followed by an increase over the later stages of married life (Rollins and Cannon, 1974; Rollins and Feldman, 1970). A problem which may militate against this, as far as musicians are concerned, is the fact that stress can increase with age, unlike in other professions, where one can expect to gain promotion and earn more as one becomes older. For the musician, it becomes more and more strenuous to be constantly expected to perform at maximum level – and with advancing age more effort is needed to achieve this. As Schulz (1981) states: 'It is the tragic lot of the musician or the performing artist in general that increased perfection is thwarted by old age as such.'

Although there is a dearth of research into the effects on family life of the musician's work, studies exist of other professions where similarly unsociable hours must be worked. For instance, Rafky (1974) carried out a survey of the wives of policemen, and this showed that one fifth to one quarter were dissatisfied with their husband's careers generally, and reported that particular aspects of the job resulted in family arguments. If further studies were to be carried out with musicians on this topic, it is quite possible that similar results would be found. At the present time, however, such studies do not exist.

Factors intrinsic to the job

Performance anxiety
Musicians and other members of the performing arts have always been aware of the problems of excessive tension and stage fright, and in recent years psychologists, physicians and other researchers have focused their attentions on the problems of the performer. Indeed, performance anxiety and related problems have been considered to be of such great importance that in 1983 the International Society for the Study of Tension in Performance was formed, with such distinguished patrons as Dame Evelyn Barbirolli, Leonard Bernstein, Sir Colin Davis and Yehudi Menuhin. Interestingly, the focus has been mainly on classical musicians, with no formal studies of performance anxiety in popular musicians.

A number of interlinked theories of performance anxiety have been put forward. For instance, Lehrer (1982) states that performance anxiety has three separately recognizable elements. These are physiological or emotional arousal, which gives rise to palpitations, perspiration and so forth; maladaptive thoughts, such as worrying about the quality of performance; and disturbances in behaviour, such as avoiding practising difficult passages. In viewing the relationship between performance and physiological arousal, the playing of an instrument bears similarities to other types of skilled behaviour, such as driving a car or playing a sport. One might assume that as arousal increases, so performance worsens accordingly, but scientific research does not confirm this idea. Rather, the relationship between tension and performance tends to follow an inverted U-shaped pattern. With increasing arousal, performance improves up to an intermediate level, and then starts to deteriorate as emotional arousal rises above the optimum. At high levels of arousal, the nervous system becomes so sensitive that too many things are responded to at the same time, and the ability to perform skilled tasks disintegrates. This pattern is known as the Yerkes–Dodson Law, and a detailed formulation of this was made by Duffy (1962). In an attempt to confirm that the inverted U pattern applies to stage performance, Steptoe (1983) carried out a study with 20 professional singers and 18 music students, and found that the relationship between emotional tension and performance quality did follow the anticipated inverted U pattern. Performance was said to be best in the setting that elicited moderate tension, with impaired performance both above and below this level.

Brantigan (1984) discusses three types of anxiety which apply to performance. These he terms reactive anxiety, adaptive anxiety and morbid anxiety. Reactive anxiety is caused by lack of skill, or inadequate preparation of a task. Adaptive anxiety is caused by the excitement which occurs in a public performance, and gives an edge to a performer's playing. Morbid anxiety has a disabling effect, and falls into two overlapping categories, namely neurotic and somatic anxiety. With neurotic anxiety, disability springs mainly from the central nervous system, and is primarily psychological in nature. It produces firstly mental and emotional immobilization, and secondly physical symptoms. The origin of somatic anxiety, on the other hand, lies primarily outside the central nervous system. It can be described as an end organ response to sympathetic stimulation, and disables the performer physically rather than psychologically, with emotional problems occurring secondarily.

Wilson (1985) proposes a three-factor model of performance anxiety. The first factor relates to the trait anxiety of the individual performer. Certain people are characteristically more sensitive than others to fear of failure and negative criticism. This may be due to low self-esteem, or an excessively reactive sympathetic nervous system, or a combination of the two. The second factor concerns the degree of task mastery that has been achieved. If a performance is intrinsically simple, or has been so well prepared that it presents no difficulties, it is much less likely to be disrupted by over-anxiety than if it is complex or under-rehearsed. Several experiments have shown that arousing and stressful conditions enhance the performance of simple, well-practised tasks, whereas conditions of emotional stress lead to less efficient performance of badly-prepared or complex tasks. These experiments are summarized by Wilson (1973). The third factor in Wilson's model focuses on the amount of situational stress which is occurring. Situations such as important concerts or auditions produce high social and environmental pressures, and the stage of over-optimal arousal is reached more rapidly.

There are now a number of studies which give empirical evidence of the extent of performance anxiety. In one revealing study, James (1984) interviewed 100 musicians who were drawn from two British regional symphony orchestras and two continental symphony orchestras. To the question, 'How does nervousness affect you?', 15 per cent said this improved their playing, while 9 per cent said it made no difference. However, 60 per cent said that it did not allow them to play as they would like, 12 per cent said that it made them lose control, and 1 per cent claimed that it ruined their playing. Surprisingly, it was found that rank-and-file players were just as likely to become anxious as section principals.

25 per cent of musicians regularly used some form of relaxation technique prior to a concert. However, they were just as likely to become anxious during a performance as their colleagues. Drug usage was low: 2 per cent always took tranquillizers, while 2 per cent always took beta blockers (drugs which act by reducing the effect of adrenalin). It was disturbing to find that 10 per cent of players always took alcohol before a performance. Two-thirds of the musicians sometimes experienced 'disturbing symptoms' during a performance. The commonest of these were rapid heart beat, increased muscle tension, sweaty hands, trembling, shaking, a sense of detachment and a loss of concentration.

In a further study, Schulz (1981) interviewed 107 members of the Vienna Symphony Orchestra. From the survey a list of stressors was placed in rank order, and the highest stressor was found to be 'nervous stress in concert'. 58 per cent of musicians rated this as a high stressor. Also, 24 per cent of musicians rated 'increased tension before performances' as a high stressor.

Several studies have been carried out to evaluate different methods of alleviating performance anxiety. James et al. (1977, 1978, 1983), James and Savage (1984), Neftel et al. (1982) and Brantigan and Brantigan (1982) have investigated the effects of beta blockers, while Kendrick et al. (1982) tested the use of cognitive therapy and behavioural therapy. Havas (1973) described her own teaching method of overcoming stage fright with special reference to violin playing. The Alexander Technique, a special method of postural retraining and muscular relaxation, has been used by Ben-Or (1983) with pianists, and by Doyle (1984) with violinists.

Good results have been reported for all these methods. Beta blockers control the somatic symptoms of anxiety, such as rise in pulse rate and trembling. However, James and Savage (1984) are of the opinion that, although beta blockers have an invaluable role to play with performers who are so incapacitated by anxiety that their livelihood is in jeopardy, ideally they should only be used as a life-line until long-term strategies for help can be worked out, and as small a dose as possible should be prescribed.

A further anxiety suffered by musicians, which is closely related to performance anxiety, is the need to attain or maintain the musical standards which they set for themselves. Piparek (1981) states that orchestra members with high artistic ambitions suffer from their more or less anonymous function in the orchestra. They are also preoccupied with a loss or decrease in their potential, and this may produce hypochondriacal reactions. Connected to this is the musician's fear of growing old, since the music profession has a set of paradoxical values regarding seniority. Whereas in most other professions, the value of a person increases with his years of experience, many instrumentalists experience a reverse evolution with advancing age. For instance, occupational diseases in wind players, such as dental or pulmonary defects, decrease the value of an elderly musician.

Thus, it can be seen that performance anxiety and related anxieties have a debilitating and widespread effect. Stage fright produces the same effects as the fight-or-flight reaction, with excess circulating catecholamines, and rises in fatty acids and triglycerides (Brantigan and Brantigan, 1982). There are thus implications for the genesis of coronary heart disease. With regard to classical musicians, several treatment strategies are now being implemented. However, this is not the case with popular musicians.

Physical stress associated with playing a musical instrument
Since each type of musical instrument differs in its form, the way it is constructed, and the way it is played, each will make different demands on its player. In other words, the demand characteristics of, for instance, the trumpet will differ from those of the piano or the double bass, and each instrument will produce its own set of stressors when an attempt is made to play it. As one example of this, Davies (1978) refers to the problems of the oboe: 'it consists of a mass of wire and metal, little springs and complicated mechanisms, and as a result oboe players are perpetually engaged in trying to keep their instruments working, since minor defects, leaks, sticking pads and other faults constantly develop'.

Samama (1985) emphasizes that every musical performance requires a great deal of physical effort, and refers to the fact that it is not at all unusual for the musician to be soaked with perspiration after every performance and to have to change his clothes. There is a widespread conviction regarding the necessity of intensive and specialized physical training for athletes, but it is only recently that it has been recognized that playing a musical instrument also demands considerable physical effort. Thus, many music teachers are now advocating exercise schedules for the physical side of music making which are as specialized as those for athletes.

The musician is subject to many ailments, and a recent editorial in the *Lancet* (1985) referred to such disorders as pianists' cramp, hornplayers' palsy, cellists' dermatitis, cor anglais players' thumb, and cymbal-players' shoulder. One of the main disorders experienced by musicians has been described by Fry (1985) as overuse injury. This can affect players of every instrument, but pianists appear to be the most frequently afflicted. Overuse injury is defined as 'a painful condition of the upper limb produced by hard, intensive use of the limb and use which is excessive for the particular individual'. The identical condition develops in other occupational fields where the hands are used intensively, for instance, with assembly-line workers in industry and with secretaries who use word processors.

In his studies in Australia, Fry (1985) found that overuse injury occurs at least in one in every twenty music school students; although he felt that a truer estimate would be one in four. In symphony orchestras where there is intense competition for jobs, the incidence of overuse injury is even higher. Overuse injuries in music students begin when the practice load is raised for examinations, assessments, competitions and recitals.

Hochberg et al. (1983) describe the problems of two outstanding American pianists, Leon Fleischer and Gary Graffman, who suffered crippling hand injuries through over-exertion. As a result of the publicity associated with these two cases, a music clinic was set up at the Massachusetts General Hospital, supervised by Dr Fred Hochberg, a neurologist, Dr Robert Leffert, an orthopaedic surgeon, and Dr Bhagwan Shahani, a neurophysiologist. More than 150 musicians, most of them pianists, have received treatment for chronic or acute tendonitis or the more serious and damaging carpal-tunnel syndrome.

Turning to the sparse literature on physical stress and popular musicians, Siegel (1983) reports that lower back problems are very frequent among drummers, since drumming relies on the ability of the player to tolerate sitting for long periods of time, while he twists the spine with a full range of motion as he plays the instrument. Chronic trauma to the spine, the insidious, cumulative degeneration of the structures of the lower back, can be created by long periods of playing with a slumping posture, which distributes the body weight in such a way that uneven stress over the vertebrae and discs precedes actual degeneration of the segments. Also relating to drummers, Ryniker (1981) states that, owing to excessively vigorous application of the foot to the bass drum pedal, a common problem is that one of the five metatarsal bones drops out of position. Continual abuse of the foot in this way leads to a need for surgery to elevate the bone back into normal position.

With regard to empirical evidence from musicians themselves, James (1984), in his study of English and continental musicians, found that one of the main factors which musicians reported as being detrimental to performance was 'problems with the instrument'. In the study of the Vienna Symphony Orchestra conducted by Schulz (1981), 31 per cent of musicians reported that 'technical problems with one's instrument' represented a high stress factor.

Thus, the physical stresses involved in playing a musical instrument may be so severe that the musician eventually finds it impossible to play. Samama (1985) states that there are many examples of this from all countries, involving all instruments.

Physical risk
Research has isolated certain high-risk occupations in terms of physical danger. For instance, Davidson and Veno (1980) carried out a survey of policemen, while Kasl (1973) isolated mine workers, soldiers and firemen as being employed in dangerous occupations. Although the threat of physical danger is not so much of a problem for the popular musician as it is for these other professions, nevertheless there are certain very real dangers. Perhaps the greatest is that from high sound-pressure levels, both in live performances and in the recording studio.

The following is a revealing comment made by the eminent record producer, George Martin:

> I continue to be astonished at the extraordinarily high levels of sound that are experienced in many control rooms. Naturally, there is excitement in hearing fine music played loudly, but it can be deceptive and, of course, physically damaging if sustained for too long.
> I make no apology for saying yet again that noise levels are too high – particularly in concerts. The levels pumped out by huge monitors are staggering and close proximity to them is bound to lead to damaged hearing. The sinister thing about impairment of hearing in this way is that its effect is often delayed by as much as four years. (Martin, 1983)

Dearing (1981) carried out an experiment to determine the sound levels achieved when the average modern drum kit is played. Dearing states that the American Occupational Safety and Health Administration (OSHA) is responsible for authorizing permissible sound levels in the workplace. Currently OSHA requires that workers be exposed no longer than eight hours to 90 dBA (dBA refers to the A-weighted decibel scale which corresponds to the ear's sensitivity). For every five dBA increase, exposure time must be cut in half. In England, the standards set by the British Occupational Hygiene Society are even more stringent. Dearing found that the recorded sound level value when the drum kit was played was 112 dBA, and notes that OSHA warns that, at levels of 115 dBA, individuals should only be exposed for fifteen minutes per day. This is indeed ominous, when one considers that modern rock concerts often consist of over two hours of continuous playing.

Martin Polon is director of Audio-Visual Services at UCLA, California. He has this to say:

> It is not uncommon to find concert environments where backstage monitoring is done with six theatre-type speaker systems and the amplifier drive is 2,000 watts. Sound levels in excess of 110 dBA are found during the entire performance. Similarly, a studio mixdown session might take as long as 24 hours, during which time the monitoring of as many as 32 tracks will take place at levels ranging from 100 to 120 dBA. Thousands of watts of amplification are found in most studios, and the trend is towards more power in most applications. (Polon, 1979)

Apart from the obvious danger to hearing from high sound levels, Polon (1979) points to other physical dangers. For instance, high volume can interfere with the cardiovascular system, causing vaso-constriction of the blood vessels, which may remain changed in size even after the high sound level has ceased. Blood pressure and heart rate may also be increased. A further disturbing finding is that high volume can be instrumental in producing chemicals in the brain usually associated with psychotic illnesses such as schizophrenia.

By its very nature, the profession of popular musician entails a great deal of travelling. The musician spends much of his time on tours, and if these take place abroad, thousands of miles will be covered, either by road or by air. Thus, by the law of averages, accidents are bound to happen, and although few statistics are available, the popular musician appears to have a high mortality rate in this regard. *Sounds* magazine (1979) published an article listing musicians who had died in road traffic accidents. Included in the list were: Duane Allman, Chris Bell, Jesse Belvin, Duster Bennett, Marc Bolan, Eddie Cochran, Johnny Horton, Johnny Kidd, Martin Lamble, Mark Leeman, J.B. Lenoir, Berry Oakley,

Mike North, Billy Stewart and Clarence White. The article also lists musicians who died in air crashes, and these include : Jim Croce, Buddy Holly, Richie Valens, the Big Bopper, four members of the Lynyrd Skynyrd group, Otis Redding and Jim Reeves. This list is not exhaustive, there are doubtless many other fatalities. Thus, travelling, which may include tightly scheduled or badly organized tours, with the concomitant factor of chronic fatigue, represents a very real danger for the popular musician.

When the musician actually arrives at the venue at which he is playing, there can be dangers involved in performing on stage, many of which result from the too-hurried setting up of equipment. Herman (1982) cites the case of Les Harvey, guitarist with the band Stone the Crows, who was killed on stage before an audience of 1,500 when he was electrocuted by his guitar. Other musicians who have died in this manner include bass player John Rostill, and vocalist Keith Relf.

Thus, the musician is exposed to a unique set of stressors with regard to physical danger.

Poor physical working conditions
Davidson and Davidson (1980) state that poor and inadequate working conditions have been found to induce frustration, impair work performance and enhance job dissatisfaction. Enclosed and isolated work environments such as the recording studio contribute significantly to feelings of isolation, time distortion, heightened emotional responses, and intensified interpersonal relationships.

Musicians often have to endure playing in poor conditions. For instance, James (1984), in his study of English and continental musicians, found that one of the main factors detrimental to performance was having to play in a cold hall. In his study of the Vienna Symphony Orchestra, Schulz (1981) found that 'inadequacies at the place of work' was rated as a high stressor by 55 per cent of musicians. This factor was second only to 'nervous stress in concert'. Heat and stale air during performances were felt to be two of the main problems. The opposite adverse effect was felt during rehearsals in unheated concert halls, with string players suffering in particular. Rated next was the problem of space: musicians had to spend their intervals in stuffy, over-crowded rooms which also served as cloakrooms. A major problem was encountered in the storage and safe-keeping of instruments. Due to a fear of damage or theft, some orchestra members did not use their privately owned precious instruments, but instead used a less valuable instrument even though they knew that the quality of instruments contributed greatly to the sound quality of the orchestra. Inadequate lighting and barely legible sheet music proved to be the worst problem for string players, with young orchestra members at a particular disadvantage, since they were less familiar with the pieces.

This study thus exemplifies the problems encountered by musicians in their place of work. Although there are no comparable studies of popular musicians, it is safe to assume that their problems are not unlike those of their classical colleagues. From anecdotal reports, other difficulties that popular musicians are likely to encounter are poor acoustics at the venue, stages too small to accommodate all the band's equipment, and venue caretakers who insist that the band leave after their engagement without adequate time to pack up their equipment.

Shift work
The musician, when playing a live engagement, typically works in the evening. Also, it is not unusual for recording sessions to take place in the evening, with all-night recording sessions being a not uncommon occurrence (Davidson and Davidson, 1980). Thus, it can be stated that the musician's work puts him in the position of the shift worker in other occupations.

Several occupational studies (including those of Cobb and Rose, 1973; Colquhoun, 1970; Hurrell and Kroes, 1975; and Selye, 1976) have concluded that shift work is a common stressor, both from an occupational and a physiological point of view. Neurophysiological rhythms such as blood sugar levels, metabolic rate, blood temperature and mental efficiency can all be affected, with the possible result of stress-related diseases. For instance, a study of air traffic controllers by Cobb and Rose (1973) found a high incidence of hypertension, mild diabetes and peptic ulcers. From an occupational point of view, studies of the police, including those of Margolis (1973) and Kroes (1976), found that shift work disrupted family life and health, and had a detrimental effect on performance on the job due to fatigue.

Piparek (1981), in his study of members of the Vienna Symphony Orchestra, notes that with the 24-hour rhythm of the nervous system, there is a switch to what he refers to as the 'trophotropic phase' at about 20.00 hours. This is the hour at which most concerts begin, and the maximum effort required contrasts sharply with the natural life rhythm. Piparek found that oversensitivity towards this unnatural concentration boost in the evening occurred mainly in the 'early risers' among his test subjects.

Although shift work can undoubtedly be stressful, Selye (1976) points out that individuals habituate to their shifts, with a consequent decrease in stress. Therefore, this factor must be borne in mind when considering shift work.

Work overload

According to French and Caplan (1972), work overload takes two forms. It is either quantitative, that is, there is too much to do, or it is qualitative, in other words, it is too complex. In a recent study of British tax inspectors, Cooper and Roden (1985) found that both qualitative and quantitative overload were predictors of high levels of anxiety and depression. With regard to the occupation of music, Davidson and Davidson (1980) make the point that time pressures are well known in recording. This is particularly so in session work, TV and radio shows. Studio time is now extremely expensive, and the pressure to complete the job can lead to feelings of overload.

A number of studies have isolated work overload as a high stress in classical musicians. In James's (1984) sample of English and continental musicians, having always to be right at a given moment (overtaxed concentration) was felt to be a high stress by 34 per cent of musicians, while other overload stresses were insufficient rehearsal (17 per cent), tiredness and overwork (13 per cent), and long hours travelling (9 per cent). In the study by Schulz (1981) of the Vienna Symphony Orchestra, the list of high stressors experienced by musicians was factor analysed, and an overload factor, which was given the name 'time spent', was extracted. This factor was made up of the following stressors: accumulated hours on duty, too many uninterrupted hours on duty, not enough leisure time, and interference with family life.

In his separate study of the Vienna Symphony Orchestra, Piparek (1981) isolated an important factor of qualitative overload. This was the need to be 'integrated completely and with utmost concentration' into the orchestra body throughout the entire performance. Piparek comments that it is difficult to maintain a prolonged state of intense concentration for more than thirty minutes, but the musician must do this throughout a two-hour performance. In addition, the musician is required to take his cue and be fully integrated into the orchestra within one hundredth of a second, a demand on precision which is almost unique in comparison to other professions.

Frequent after-effects of the intense concentration of performance were feelings of mental exhaustion, reduced ability to remember, desire for solitude, irritability and sleep disturbance. One interesting but frequently distressing after-effect was the inability to 'get a tune out of one's head'. Some musicians are what

Piparek terms 'acoustic eidetics', and remember tunes with almost hallucinatory clearness.

Although no studies exist, popular musicians undoubtedly have comparable problems to the above.

Person–environment fit and job satisfaction
Person–environment fit has been defined by McMichael (1978) as an interaction between an individual's psychosocial characteristics and the objective environmental work conditions. Stress or 'misfit' occurs either when the demand of the job exceeds the person's capability, or when the person's capability exceeds the demand of the job.

Interestingly, although the musicians in the studies of both James (1984) and Schulz (1981) reported several sources of stress, they nevertheless experienced a high degree of job satisfaction. In James's (1984) study, 91 per cent of players said that their career made them happy, while in the study by Schulz (1981), 84 per cent of players said they were satisfied in their work. One specific source of discontent was that the artistic potential of the orchestra was not being properly realized. 55 per cent of players stated that they were not satisfied with the prestige of the orchestra. These musicians probably had high job satisfaction because they were playing music which they enjoyed.

One important source of person–environment misfit for musicians is highlighted in a survey by Becker (1963). This was a sociological study of dance band musicians who experienced a high degree of frustration because they were compelled to play commercial dance music in order to earn a living, when they really wished to play jazz, which was artistically satisfying but not lucrative. There were two sources of frustration: the music they had to play, and the lack of understanding of the musicians' aspirations by their audience.

This study pinpoints an important problem for the popular musician. For financial reasons, he frequently has to play music that is unstimulating and unchallenging, often in the setting of theatre shows, pantomimes and summer seasons, with consequent feelings of boredom and frustration. This person–environment misfit situation is thus of the type whereby the person's capability exceeds the demand of the job.

Career development

According to Cooper and Marshall (1976), there are a number of potential stressors in the area of career development. These include, lack of job security, fear of redundancy, thwarted ambition, under-promotion, and frustration at having reached one's career ceiling. Certain stress outcomes have been found to be related to these factors. For instance, Erickson et al. (1972) found that lack of job advancement was related to the incidence of psychiatric disorders.

The musician appears to be particularly prone to stresses relating to career development. As Piparek (1981) states, age is often a crucial stress factor. In most professions, a person's value increases with his years of experience, but a musician's age may militate against him, as he becomes more subject to physical illness and is thus less able to perform. Music is indeed in many ways a young man's profession. With regard to lack of job security, Raeburn (1984), in her study of occupational stress in rock musicians, found that job insecurity, lack of financial support, and lack of recognition from the music industry were three of the most frequently and intensively experienced stressors.

Possibly one of the most revealing accounts of the stresses which the popular musician must face in attempting to develop his career is contained in the book *The Jazz Life* by Nat Hentoff (1961). Bearing in mind the fact that this was written at the beginning of the 1960s, and relates mainly to black American jazz musicians, it nevertheless contains a great deal of information which illustrates the sorts of things that popular musicians as a whole still have to cope with.

Hentoff describes what happens when the aspiring jazz musician arrives in New York. He may have made a reputation in another city, but New York is the mecca of the jazz world, containing the cream of jazz musicians, and he must start once more from the bottom and prove himself to his peers. This can be extremely stressful, and some musicians do not pass the test.

The New York Musicians' Union contains 30,000 members, and of these, only about 3,000 work regularly. For a musician who is not a native New Yorker, it takes six months to be fully admitted to the New York Musicians' Union. As well as this, he must apply for a police permit in order to work in establishments where alcohol is sold. Having overcome these obstacles, the musician then begins his search for work.

Hentoff cites the case of Julian Adderley, a jazz musician from Florida who gained acceptance in New York. He formed a five-piece band, which began working for 1,000 dollars per week. Out of this was taken 150 dollars manager's commission, 75 dollars in union taxes, 125 dollars in federal with-holding taxes, plus petrol and hotel bills. The band made records, but received no recording royalties. Although it was artistically successful, it was still earning only 1,000 dollars per week at the end of twenty months, and was 9,000 dollars in debt. Adderley was forced to break the band up. He was fortunate, since, because his personal reputation as a musician had become enhanced, he was offered a job with a famous and established musician, Miles Davis.

Shearlaw (1984) describes the stresses which the members of an unknown rock band must endure when commencing their careers. In order to make the band's name known, one-night engagements, residencies and small-scale tours must be played. Touring is a combination of hard work, luck, and an ability to survive on virtually no money. If the band manage to survive and progress, they will have to employ several people, including a manager, a sound engineer and a road crew. If the band actually arrive at the stage of having a record in the hit parade, this is no guarantee of financial reward or long-term success. It is not unknown for a band to have a hit record while still being paid a mere £35 each per week. A band may wish to further its career by supporting a famous band on a large-scale tour, but it is not uncommon for the support band to be obliged to pay for the privilege. This practice is known as the 'buy-on'. A band with a number of hit records might charge up to £7,000 as a buy-on.

At the other end of the scale, success may bring about the phenomenon of 'reaching the top too soon', with all its accompanying pressures. In describing this, Black (1984b) states that success as a rock musician involves an endless round of touring, recording, interviews, song-writing and public appearances. Total disorientation and psychological breakdown can be the end result.

Black (1984b) makes the important point that although the lifestyle of a rock musician brings immense pressures and temptations, the music industry makes no official recognition of this fact, and takes no responsibility.

Career development and female popular musicians
In occupational stress research, there has been a recent emphasis on the special problems encountered by women in the working environment, for instance in the study of women managers by Cooper and Davidson (1982). Although there has always been a place for the female vocalist, popular music, like classical music, has been dominated by male instrumentalists. This is probably due, in part, to the views of Western culture, which deem that it is undignified for a woman to play an instrument, and which were expressed by the Italian diplomat and philosopher Baldassare Castiglione, who in 1528 wrote:

> Imagine with yourself what an unsightly matter it were to see a woman play upon a tabour or a drum, or blow in a flute or trumpet, or any like instrument; and this is because the boisterousness of them doth both cover and take away that sweet mildness which setteth so forth every deed that a woman doeth. (Dahl, 1984)

Although the lack of women instrumentalists in popular music may be due partly to male prejudice, it is important to consider other reasons. The 'social limitation' hypothesis of lack of creative output in women is not the only way of looking at this area. Tyler (1965) states that even in traditionally female pursuits such as hairdressing, cookery and needlework, it is men who are most frequently the innovators and leaders. Maccoby (1966) refers to a study in which a sample of female academics at Radcliffe College was compared with a sample of male academics who were equal in status and qualifications. The women produced 'substantially less' academic publications, and this was regardless of discipline or their domestic commitments. It is possible that men are more frequently able to think in a creative way, and also possess greater motivation to actualize their ideas. However, this suggestion can only be tentative.

Findings from research indicate that women who enter creative professions tend to have more 'masculine' characteristics. Gotz and Gotz (1979a,b), in a study of professional artists, found that female artists scored much higher than female non-artists on the psychoticism dimension of the Eysenck Personality Questionnaire, indicating that they were more tough-minded. In a study of the significance of sex differences in the personality of the musician, Kemp (1982) concluded that psychologically androgynous females appear to be the best endowed with the wider range of temperaments necessary for success in the field of music.

Whatever the reasons for the lack of female instrumentalists, women who do enter the popular music profession have encountered difficulties. The jazz musician Marjorie Hyams states:

> In a sense, you weren't really looked upon as a musician, especially in clubs. There was more interest in what you were going to wear or how your hair was fixed – they just wanted you to look attractive, ultra-feminine, largely because you were doing something they didn't consider feminine. Most of the time I just fought it and didn't listen to them. Only in retrospect, when you start looking back and analysing, you can see the obstacles that were put in front of you. I just thought at the time that I was too young to handle it, but now I see that it was really rampant chauvinism. (Dahl, 1984)

At the present time, perhaps partly due to the feminist movement, more women are entering popular music, not only as instrumentalists, but also in other capacities such as that of record producer. Steward and Garratt (1984), in an admittedly feminist treatment, state that the music business is one of the world's largest leisure industries, but it is bent on keeping women out of all but the most traditional roles. Carol Colman, a bass player with a well-known pop group, and also a trainee record producer, is quoted as saying:

> You have to be twice as smart, twice as tough, and twice as good as the men just to get to the bottom of the rank where you can eat and pay your rent. (Steward and Garratt, 1984)

There is thus evidence from popular and anecdotal sources that women experience obstacles to career development in popular music. This would prove a fruitful area for future academic research.

Relationships at work

Poor relationships with one's work colleagues have been implicated in job stress. Also included are relationships with subordinates and superiors. In a study by Caplan et al. (1975), it was found that social support from colleagues served to relieve work pressures. It was also shown to condition the effect of job stress on glucose, blood pressure, cortisone and the number of cigarettes smoked.

In studies of classical musicians, one of the main sources of stress has been found to be the musician's relationship with his superior, that is the conductor. In the study by James (1984), having a bad conductor was found to be the highest stressor for British musicians, with 57 per cent of subjects rating this a high stressor. In this study, musicians frequently and spontaneously commented that British conductors are vastly overpaid, incompetent, vindictive and arrogant.

In Schulz's (1981) study, conductors were also found to be a problem. 27 per cent of orchestra musicians stated that they found it to be very stressful coping with the different methods used by conductors. The study by Piparek (1981) showed that orchestra musicians have a strong psychological dependence upon the conductor, and they suffer if he does not exhibit sound qualities of leadership. In popular music, the equivalent of the conductor is the bandleader or the musical director. Although no studies exist, it is highly probable that similar problems occur between popular musicians and their bandleaders.

In all the above studies, there was evidence of tension in the musician's relationships with his colleagues. In the studies by James (1984) and Piparek (1981), criticisms of one's musical performance by colleagues was a source of stress, and in Piparek's study this criticism was found to be more stressful than that from members of the audience or from press reviews. The study by Schulz (1981) gives some interesting insights into the social tensions in an orchestra. 60 per cent of the musicians stated that envy is an integral part of the musician's profession, while 36 per cent said that they had personal enemies in the orchestra. It was found that high artistic prestige as a musician was a very highly rated quality, and this correlated significantly with popularity as a person. The majority of friendships within an orchestra were found to exist within the musician's own instrument group, with the brass players being the most isolated group. This finding tends to be confirmed in the study by Davies (1978), where string players described brass players as being oafish, uncouth and loud-mouthed. The brass players, for their part, described string players as being precious, oversensitive, touchy and humourless.

In a study by Bayer (1982), a large sample of American orchestral musicians filled in a questionnaire relating to various stresses. From statistical analysis, it was found that one of the main predictors of both poor physical health and poor psychological outcomes was 'having problems with one's partner on the stand'. There is thus evidence that classical musicians experience stresses in their relationships at work, and it is not unlikely that popular musicians find themselves in a similar position.

Organizational structure and climate

Being part of a business or industrial organization carries its own intrinsic stresses. The individual may feel threatened in terms of his identity, autonomy and freedom. Criticisms which are frequently levelled at organizations by individuals are that they are not allowed enough participation in decision-making processes, and suffer from lack of effective consultation and communication. They may be subjected to office politics, and may feel that their behaviour is restricted, for instance by budgets (Cooper and Marshall, 1976, 1978). Certain studies, including those of French and Caplan (1972) and Margolis et al. (1974), found that when organization members had greater participation in decision-making, there was an increase in productivity and performance, and levels of physical and mental health improved.

For the popular musician, one of the main types of organization in which he will be involved is the band or orchestra. For instance, if he is a member of a radio orchestra, he is employed by the radio company, and if he is a member of a theatre orchestra he may sign a contract for the duration of the particular theatre show for which he is playing. It is not unusual for members of an orchestra to be dissatisfied with its organizational structure. For instance, in the study by Schulz (1981), 67 per cent of musicians felt there was a need for changes in their employment contracts, 60 per cent felt there was a need for more efficient management of the orchestra, and 50 per cent desired a greater participation in decision-making with regard to musical problems. In the study by Piparek (1981), 55 per cent of musicians complained that they did not have any choice with regard to conductors or concert programmes. It was felt that, with regard to programmes, good compositions were often neglected in favour of those by controversial composers supported by influential lobbies.

In the broader sense, there is a much larger organization in which the popular musician will become involved, especially if he is a member of a pop or rock band. This is the popular music business, which is a multimillion pound, worldwide industry. At a conservative estimate, the rock business worldwide at the present time has a turnover of roughly £16 billion per year, including income from all the other industries like radio, music magazines, television, films and printing, which earn large revenues from rock's side-products. In order to understand better the stresses to which the popular musician may be subjected as part of this organization, it is helpful to look in more detail at the complexities of the music business.

Black (1984a) states that first of all, it is essential for a band to have a good manager. No band will survive without one. Next, the band must have a good lawyer, who will negotiate the band's contract with the manager, agents, promoters, music publishers and record companies. At least one member of the band should understand contracts as much as the lawyer. A not uncommon stress to which the popular musician is subjected is the phenomenon of 'being ripped off'. Black (1984a) cites the case of the group Wham, who found themselves earning no more than £100 per week at a time when their records were at the top of album and singles charts worldwide. Included in their contract were clauses which actually reduced their royalty payments by half if their records were advertised on television, and which gave them no royalties on the sales of 12" singles.

The musician must understand the complexities of record royalties and song copyrights, and should be a member of the Musicians' Union, a trade organization which fights for the rights of musicians. One extremely stressful factor lies in the area of tax payments. For instance, an inexperienced band may have several hit records in a short period and then, for some reason, stop having hits. They may find that no one has been paying tax for them, and thus face huge tax demands, possibly fines for neglect or wilful default, and interest charges backdated to the first day on which tax fell due.

The stress of the 'artist versus businessman' clash may occur typically between the band and the record company. Hrano (1984) states that the simple motive of record companies is to make money, and therefore what they expect from a band, among other things, is that they will produce excellent records which will sell. The band must be prepared to cooperate with their aims and objectives. Thus, a great deal of acrimony is the frequent result: the musician wishes to be creative, and the record executive wishes to make a profit. Wright (1983), himself a record executive, states that one of the main problems with the music business at the present time is that it has become too formalized. Because of the profit motive, creative executives are dismissed, and power passes to accountants and lawyers, who then sign up artists and make records with the sole intention of pandering to the existing demand from radio stations. Chances are thus missed on more creative artists. Thus, the musician may come to feel like an anonymous cog in a huge business machine, with typically stressful feelings of loss of identity, autonomy and freedom.

Evidence of this is provided in the study of occupational stress in rock musicians by Raeburn (1984), where two of the most frequently and intensively experienced stressors were 'lack of recognition from the music industry', and 'pressure to produce a certain quality of product'.

Stress outcomes

Stress-related illnesses such as coronary heart disease have been increasing in both the United States and Great Britain in the past twenty years. Cooper (1980a) states that in Great Britain the death rate in males between the ages 35 to 44 doubled between the years 1950 and 1973. This increase was much more rapid than that in older age ranges, and by 1973, 41 per cent of deaths in the age group 35 to 44 were due to cardiovascular disease. Davidson and Cooper (1981) highlight the fact that there has been an increase in other problems, which are probably manifestations of stress. These include alcoholism, industrial accidents and short-term illnesses. It was estimated in the United States in 1976 that the loss of working days cost £55 million solely in social security benefit payments. Cooper and Marshall (1978) state that there is much evidence implicating occupational stress in the genesis of stress-related illnesses like heart disease.

*Occupational stress and physical illnesses
in musicians*

Carruthers (1980) feels that although there is still some controversy surrounding the connection between occupational stress and heart disease, psychophysiological studies of airline pilots, racing car drivers and public speakers give evidence of such a connection.

Haider and Groll-Knapp (1981) carried out a psychophysiological study of 24 members of the Vienna Symphony Orchestra. In order to determine circulatory stress, electrocardiogram readings were continuously recorded during rehearsals and concerts. It was found that, during concerts, the maximum pulse rate for musicians overall was 120 beats per minute. However, individual musicians reached maximum pulse rates of over 150 beats per minute. Anticipation of an entrance into a difficult musical passage led to a sharp increase in pulse rate, and this was felt to constitute severe circulatory stress. The term 'exertional pulse rate' is sometimes used to describe the increase in pulse rate compared to pulse rate when at rest, and is a measure of the stress which can accompany an activity. Certain musicians exhibited an increase of 50 beats per minute compared to their pulse rate at rest. Haider and Groll-Knapp (1981) conclude that musicians suffer high levels of circulatory stress during concerts, and that this could lead to cardio-circulatory disorders.

Reference has already been made to other physical illnesses to which musicians may be prone, with a high incidence of overuse injury being reported (Fry, 1985), and the consequent opening of the Massachusetts music clinic (Hochberg et al., 1983). Other evidence of occupationally induced injuries comes from a study by Abelin et al. (1962). String players were found to suffer from necrotic damage to arms and fingers, dermatitis and pachymenia of the neck, and cramps in fingers and arms. In wind players, an overstraining in the lips was reported, with pain, irritation and inflammation.

Reference has also been made to the high sound levels to which musicians can be subjected, with the result of possible permanent hearing impairment. Haider and Groll-Knapp (1981) measured sound levels during six frequently performed pieces of music, and found that for all the pieces, the maximum sound levels were above 100 dBA. For pieces by Ravel and Rachmaninov, maximum sound levels reached 127 dBA. Haider and Groll-Knapp comment that these are sound values where one has to expect autonomic reactions including reduction of pulse amplitudes. In this sound intensity range, furthermore, damage to the inner ear must be expected from long-term, continuous effects.

There is thus some evidence that musicians may be prone to a variety of physical disorders.

Occupational stress and psychological health in musicians

Schuler (1980) states that the variables which are used most frequently to represent psychological symptoms of stress include tension, anxiety, depression, boredom and psychological fatigue. Russek and Zohman (1958) suggested that psychological symptoms preceded physiological symptoms, and Margolis et al. (1974) were of the opinion that stress leads to five types of strain. These are: short-term subjective conditions such as anxiety; long-term chronic symptoms such as depression; transient physiological changes such as blood pressure; physical illness such as heart disease or ulcers; and work performance changes.

Reference has previously been made to findings which suggest that musicians overall tend to have anxiety-prone personalities (Kemp, 1981), and that performance anxiety is a major problem for musicians (Brantigan, 1984), to such an extent that several anxiety-management strategies have been implemented (for example, James et al., 1983, Brantigan and Brantigan, 1982, Ben-Or, 1983).

Haider and Groll-Knapp (1981), in their investigation of stress experienced by musicians while performing in concert, measured electrical activity of the brain using electroencephalogram readings. It was found that readings gave evidence of a dominance by beta waves, often over a long duration. Any alpha waves that occurred lasted only briefly, and slow potential shifts and expectancy waves indicated anticipatory stress. In a normal state of relaxed wakefulness, alpha waves occur and when mental activity takes place these are replaced by beta waves, normally for short periods. Haider and Groll-Knapp (1981) therefore conclude that long-lasting stress on the central nervous system was demonstrated by EEG readings. During the musicians' performance there was virtually a complete lack of alpha waves, indicating ongoing mental effort and high arousal.

As previously noted, Piparek (1981) found that the intense concentration of musical performance produced after-effects in musicians such as mental exhaustion, disturbed memory function, desire for solitude, irritability and sleep disturbance.

It therefore appears, at least from the evidence of studies with classical musicians, that the musician's work may give rise to a number of stress-induced psychological outcomes.

Alcoholism in musicians

Between 1966 and 1974, admissions to alcoholism units in British hospitals increased from under 6,000 to over 8,000 (Cooper, 1980). By 1985, the direct costs of alcohol abuse to UK industry was £1.4 billion. In a study in the United States, Margolis et al. (1974) interviewed over 1,500 workers in a variety of occupations. It was found that a variety of work stressors were implicated in escapist drinking. A study of the police force by Davidson and Veno (1980) suggested that, in order to cope with work stress, some members of the profession resorted to heavy drinking.

The academic literature on alcohol abuse in musicians is sparse. However, James (1984) found that, in his study of English and continental musicians, 10 per cent of players always took alcohol before a performance in order to calm their nerves. Davies (1978) concurs with these findings. In interviews, several musicians described the classical music scene in London as being especially competitive and stressful, and claimed that there was a relationship between this fact and the heavy drinking of many principal musicians.

Drug abuse in musicians

A particularly important question to try to answer in the context of this chapter is: how prevalent is the use of 'hard' drugs such as heroin among popular musicians? This question is important because it is one which appears to be of great interest to members of the general public, and because it is the frequent focus of reports in the media. A further question which arises is that if musicians are involved in the abuse of drugs, how much is this a result of the stresses of their profession?

The connection between narcotics and popular music appears to have been made specifically with regard to American modern jazz in the years after the Second World War (Hentoff, 1961). Hentoff puts forward the theory that modern jazz was a revolutionary music which was rejected by the general public. Like the music, heroin was defiantly anti-establishment. The comments of the jazz musician Gerry Mulligan illuminate this further:

> In the late 1940s, just making a living was rough. . . . These were the days of widespread general use of junk around town (New York). . . . There was a frustration everywhere with us. Nobody really seemed to know what they were doing or where they were going. Junk could provide a dream world. The daily process of living was dull, and you had to scrounge for an income when you just wanted to play your horn. Junk seemed to help in a bad time. (Hentoff, 1961)

A different aspect of the problem is given by the jazz musician Bob Brookmeyer:

> No form of music is as intense emotionally for the man making it as jazz. It is an immediate, sensate emotion that does not last . . . it's a thrill exceeded only by making love . . . some guys try to prolong that feeling of ecstasy . . . there's also a fraternity among some of those who are addicted that satisfies a need for togetherness. Life can be pretty purposeless for a jazz musician. You lose a feeling of being an accepted part of society. There's a need to be one at least with your own group. (Hentoff, 1961)

Thus, although there is a dearth of statistical and academic information, it is possible to glean certain facts regarding drug abuse and popular musicians. Narcotics addiction was prevalent among modern jazz musicians in the United States in the period after the Second World War, and appears to have come about at least partly as a result of stressful factors in the musician's lifestyle. Due to the unacceptability of his music, the musician suffered from feelings of alienation and found it difficult to make a living. Also, he sometimes felt the need to sustain a sense of heightened emotional arousal, created by music, by taking drugs.

Winick (1959) carried out a survey of the use of drugs by a group of American jazz musicians. 357 subjects between the ages of 18 and 57 were interviewed. With regard to marijuana, 82 per cent had used it at least once, 54 per cent were occasional users, and 23 per cent were regular users. With regard to heroin, 53 per cent had used it at least once, 24 per cent used it occasionally, and 16 per cent were regular users. Heroin use was concentrated in the age group 25 to 39, after which it fell off to very little.

Hentoff (1961) is of the opinion that as modern jazz grew older and more accepted, and as younger players saw outstanding musicians die or experience problems due to drugs, heroin addiction became far less widespread. It would appear that this decrease in use among jazz musicians has continued up to the present time.

With regard to rock and pop musicians, Herman (1982) feels that drugs can be a necessary form of sustenance when involved in arduous work schedules, unsociable hours and the high expectations of audiences. John Lennon is quoted as saying that the only way to survive in Hamburg in the early 1960s when playing for eight hours per night was to take amphetamines. Discussing the rigours of touring, Herman (1982) states that a sense of unfamiliarity and isolation is produced in the context of very hard work, resulting in feelings of disorientation. By the mid 1970s, the rock music business had become strongly linked to the drug trade, and it was estimated that 90 per cent of all cocaine use in the United States centred on the rock and film industries. A list of rock musicians who died either as a direct or indirect result of drug abuse includes the names Janis Joplin, Brian Jones, Jimi Hendrix, Tim Hardin, Mike Bloomfield, Robbie Mackintosh, Tommy Bolin, Lowell George, Paul Kossoff, Jimmy McCulloch, Gram Parsons and Sid Vicious.

It thus appears that there is evidence of drug abuse due to the stresses of the musician's occupation. However, few statistics are available, and a further factor to take into consideration is that, unless a musician has attained a higher income bracket, he may not be able to afford to buy drugs. It is probably true to say that the majority of musicians are not in this higher income bracket.

Conclusions

This chapter has attempted to review the literature which is relevant to occupational stress in professional popular musicians. Certain stressors stand out as having particular relevance for the popular musician. These are:

1 Performance anxiety.
2 Problems associated with playing a musical instrument.
3 Physical danger, including problems associated with playing in a context of high sound levels.
4 For musicians who play specifically in rock and pop bands, problems associated with organizational structure. The organization in this case is the pop music business, a multimillion pound, worldwide industry.

In the classical field, psychological and physical tension associated with playing is felt to be such a problem that an international society has been set up in order to further research and treatment strategies. No such organization exists for popular musicians.

The following chapters describe the first attempt at a large-scale study of popular musicians, with a specific emphasis on isolating stressors and stress outcomes.

4
Sources of stress in rock, pop, jazz and commercial music

In order to investigate the major sources of stress experienced by British professional popular musicians, we spent over a year carrying out in-depth interviews with 70 male popular musicians based both in London and the North of England. Several were freelance musicians and worked in all areas of popular music, including jazz, rock, pop and dance music, while others specialized in a particular field such as jazz or rock. Certain musicians concentrated their work on recording sessions, while others were involved mainly in live gigs. Some were very well known in their own right, and some were or had been members of well-known bands, but the majority comprised everyday working musicians. Ages ranged from 22 to 62, with a mean age of 40. The sample comprised 16 brass players (10 trumpeters and 6 trombonists), 13 saxophonists, 11 keyboard players, 10 guitarists, 10 bass players and 10 drummers.

Each interview, which was tape-recorded and lasted over two hours, covered the items which had been identified as being of importance in the review of the literature relating to musicians and stress. Each musician was also asked to complete the Eysenck Personality Questionnaire (Eysenck and Eysenck, 1975), since no previous personality studies of professional popular musicians existed, and since personality is an important variable in the reaction to stress (Davidson and Cooper, 1981).

This chapter, then is devoted mainly to popular musicians talking, often eloquently and pungently, about the stresses of their work. The data from the completion of the Eysenck Personality Questionnaire is also discussed.

Performance anxiety and related anxieties

As emerged in the literature review, performance anxiety is one of the major problems which can face the performing artist. Our interview sample discussed this topic at length, and the following comments from a freelance musician are typical:

> Over the past three years I've been suffering increasingly from nervous

tension at work. Initially it started as a looseness of the bowels – at first I didn't know whether it was stomach trouble causing bad nerves or vice-versa. I now tend to think that it is nervousness causing bad stomachs. I am now at the stage where I find it extremely difficult to do 'live' gigs at all. Recording sessions don't bother me at all, hardly. However, I can usually control it to a certain extent, but on one occasion I couldn't and I had fast heartbeat, difficulty in breathing, shaking and sweating. In other words, sheer panic. Since then I have tried not to do 'live' gigs at all. Theatre pit work is not so bad, but the only thing I can say I *enjoy* doing is playing tuba in trad. bands, but I'm sometimes bothered, even so.

My doctor has given me some Ativan pills but I don't like them, so I flushed them down the toilet. Since then he gave me some Anxon pills which I find better, but no answer to the problem really.

I am fortunately able to earn some money doing some upholstery, but some days I get a bit nervous with that.

I was drinking very heavily until six months ago (six or eight pints of bitter a day and a few port and brandys) but I've kept to two or three pints of bitter a day and no shorts at all since then. I feel much better usually, because of this. But, for instance, I've got the Inland Revenue after me and I can't pay them, and this has tended to set the trouble off again. I sometimes think I'm heading for a breakdown; but I hope I can prevent that.

A well-known jazz musician had this to say:

I think I experienced in some depth the very special problems of the professional musician. In fact, for a long time, practical manifestations of all kinds of stress made it nearly impossible for me to either play my instrument or walk upright in the street. During three unhappy years living in London, I had all kinds of illnesses, including tachycardia, extreme depression, and a nervous complaint for which I was treated, or at least examined, by four private doctors, the London Hospital, and a psychoanalyst. The complaint made it impossible for me to travel in tubes, to drive, or to stand alone in an open space. For a time this made performance virtually impossible too, of course.

I moved back home to a place of my own, with a secure domestic situation, and a mantlepiece – paid for – to put my feet on. I'm now happier, but the stress would, I know, have probably killed me, or at least put me in a mental ward, in ten years.

This musician attempted to explain the causes of his anxiety state. He felt that the lifestyle of a jazz musician is often divorced from everyday reality, and he expressed his feelings as follows:

I found myself gradually not really communicating with anyone. In a stressful self-employed world with the phone constantly ringing, con-tinual often selfish demands on your time by bookers/musicians and so on, this is bad news, and I watched my personality change, much for the worse. I was constantly wracked by imaginings of bad health, fear of attack by others, stress from the inevitable and often deliberate pressures asserted by other musicians.

Against this, I began to realise that the jazz world was neither interested, nor understanding. Musicians, for the most part, are basically interested just in performance. Most other life patterns are really secondary. So no real chance to unburden there. Promoters – your usual business associates – have no interest in musicians as people, apart from the general gratification of their image of what a musician is *supposed* to be like. Depart from this image, often at your peril . . .

So life can easily go on, day by day, until you die. The assertion of, and even belief in proper human values can easily go by the board, when there's nothing in your day-by-day life to encourage belief in them. You need either to be very strong – or perhaps stupid – to resist them. No wonder that a great many elderly or even middle-aged musicians are either prematurely totally disenchanted, or in a few cases, totally self-deluding. Imagine the psychological trauma that could attend being fêted as someone very famous, once a month in a tiny club by fifty people. After fifty years' service you may like to believe them, and have only to face the contradiction of a several-thousand-pound overdraft when you wake up next morning, and otherwise total obscurity.

The musician has often nothing but a few highly fallible standards to adhere to, and a world to relate to that is basically created – at least until recently – by a few part-time enthusiasts to indulge their spare-time fantasies. I was able to discover two home truths (1) that the world of professional jazz is too fragile to put all your faith in and (2) that the falseness of the life can, if unmonitored, crack you to pieces.

Another musician highlighted the special anxieties involved in working in recording sessions:

I am a freelance session player, although I do work regularly for a number of bands/artistes, and receive regular bookings from certain companies.

I find the pressures of running myself as a small business are by far the most frightening. I lack the relative safety of being part of a large organization, such as a 'staff' orchestra (BBC etc. . . .) or a band signed to management, record companies etc. . . .

However, the benefits of being freelance tend to outweigh the problems caused; I don't have to rely on the punctuality (or not!) of irresponsible rock musicians! I can choose to a certain extent the styles of music I wish to play, and filter out some of the many charlatans and crooks who are so abundant in the entertainment business.

In general I would say that I don't regret becoming a musician, but it is a life fraught with pressures (particularly for the young and inexperienced; I had a peptic ulcer at 21), and the average span of a musician's active life is short.

When you're in the recording studio, you're expected to be able to deliver perfection. You keep one eye on the studio clock, knowing that any mistakes or delays are costing the studio money. You're only as good as your last gig, and you worry whether you've come up to expectations.

An important aspect of performance anxiety concerns the need to reach or maintain self-imposed standards of musicianship, and this subject was raised frequently by the interview sample. It is interesting to note that this is an internally imposed, rather than an externally imposed source of stress, and it undoubtedly manifests itself in anyone involved in a so-called 'creative' pursuit, such as an actor, artist, novelist or comedian. Research into creativity (see, for instance, Cattell and Butcher, 1968; Mackinnon, 1962) has shown that the creative personality often prefers to think through problems alone, depending on self-sufficiency and independence. Some of the musicians' own comments illustrate graphically the nature of this particular stressor:

> I'd just be content playing in a creative environment and earning a living. I just want to progress as a musician.

> If you've got high standards, you're trying to keep up to them all the time.

> You have your own standards to keep up to, and you know that all eyes are on you. I get upset if I think I've made a mess of something.

> I made a positive decision to do gigs that I would find creative and musically rewarding. It's hard facing up to shortcomings in your playing. I'm very ambitious on a creative level. I don't want financial reward. I'm always setting goals for myself.

> I don't want fame and fortune, but I want a good reputation in the music business. There's a constant pressure to keep up your standard. I won't play music that's really bad. It ruins your reputation.

One famous jazz musician, whose playing is highly regarded, described at length his extreme degree of self-criticism, and his consequent mental anguish:

> I've had my moments, but I'm nowhere near the player I'd like to be. I don't suppose anybody is – and it's just a continual drag, really. Any musician will tell you that playing is 95 per cent a pain in the arse, a frustration, and 5 per cent you feel okay about. I was talking to Dizzy Gillespie about it, and I said: 'Do you feel that you play within certain confined channels most of the time, and now and again the channels seem to broaden out and something'll really happen?' And he said: 'Yeah'. So I said: 'Well, how often do you feel that it really happens?' and he said 'Once a year if I'm lucky'. That's from Dizzy Gillespie. You get on stage, and somehow, I don't know, 50 per cent of your technique seems to have disappeared. You find yourself stumbling and fumbling over things that you *know* you can play, and it just seems to fly out the window.

> *You* are your only worthwhile critic. Once you have played, and feel that you've played something worthwhile – you're happy about it, and feel like you've created something – after that, it's a pain if it's not approaching that kind of standard. Quite right – I'd probably hear John Coltrane on a bad night – for him – and I would think it was amazing. So it *is* kind of comparative, but it's really no consolation – it doesn't help. Playing an instrument seriously – I mean, you've got that cross to bear, really, all the time you're a player.

I'm very open to vibes. I find these things very affecting. I only have to look in a room where I'm playing and see someone who I think isn't sympathetic to the way I play, then that's me finished, you know? I mean, I'm talking about another musician. It may be imagination, but it has an effect, so it's a great help if you feel there's a sympathetic audience.

In the studio, when the red light goes on and you've got to turn it on – I can't. With me, it's not a question of being scared of the red light, it's – well, jazz music is improvised and spontaneous, and it's *fleeting* really, and you can't create to order – it's impossible.

A broadly based anxiety from which the popular musician suffers is caused by the ignorance of the public, and the low esteem in which society generally holds popular music. One respected jazz musician was able to temper with humour his feelings about the public. He said:

I find it stressful when idiots ask stupid questions like 'Do you like working with Oscar Peterson?' When I say, 'No, I hate it!' they look at me as if I'm crazy. Can't they realize that this is probably the best gig of my life! I also dislike people who think that music isn't a real job. I tell them I'm a brain surgeon during the day!

One rock musician with many years of experience behind him expounded passionately and at length on this subject:

Most people regard musicians as one step up the 'social ladder' from rapists and muggers, and it's this 'alienation' from the non-musician that I believe creates most of the problems. The prolonged experience of being regarded as 'unclean' by 'civilians' is what causes the musician to retreat into himself, and causes a build-up of neuroses which can all-too-easily lead to a nervous breakdown. This is compounded by many facts.

1 Musicians find little backing: they can be robbed virtually indiscriminately.
2 Musicians belong to the only Union I know of where a huge percentage are *semi-pro*, and only do it for beer money. Can you see Arthur Scargill standing for that?
3 If a musician needs help from his government, he frequently finds it withheld. He can't get dole because he's self-employed, he can't fill in the forms because he doesn't 'fit' the questions. He can't go to the Job Centre for a gig to suit his skills. In short, if you're a musician, you don't qualify. Except, of course, at tax time!
4 There is no standard set. The public wouldn't know a good player from a bad one, the media largely promote mediocrity, and the Musicians' Union have no set standard to conform to: pay your subs., and you're in! In any other profession, it's a fair bet that as you become more skilful, you move up, and do better quality work. Not so for the musician.
5 The public judge a musician *only* by the money he earns. If he's rich, he's a great man. If he's poor, he's a time-wasting parasite who should

get a 'real' job. This has unfortunate repercussions. Bear with a little story. There once was a band who had about 18 hit records including four or five number ones. Because they were being legally robbed, however, they had no money. Now the band have split up, the guitarist (*not me*, I'd better make clear), is a skint musician and will most surely be treated as such. He is the victim. The *perpetrator* of this deed has a luxury yacht, five or six houses in various parts of the world, and is treated with forelock-tugging respect. This is the world of the musician.

All this is allowed to go on because the public is totally ignorant of it. All their information is gleaned from the *Melody Maker* and Radio One. No-one has ever seriously tried to explain the music profession to them. They think it is easy; they think it is impure; they think it is pointless; they think it is drug-ridden; they think it is worthless.

Even despite the purely economic fact that Elton John has probably paid more tax than Wigan, and brought in more foreign earnings that British Steel, it is not a 'real' job!

Musicians in the interview sample therefore provided evidence that several aspects of performance anxiety and related anxieties can be highly stressful, concurring with previous studies referred to in the literature review.

Work overload

A large percentage of musicians rated work overload as being highly stressful. Although work may be sporadic, when it does come, it can be intensive. It may involve, for instance, working at a recording session during the day, which may start early in the morning, and then playing on a live gig in the evening, which may finish in the early hours. Or it may involve touring, which may last between a few days and a month, or even longer, with the necessity of extensive travelling. Typical comments on work overload were as follows:

A major stress is the lack of sleep, due to recording sessions during the day and gigs at night. This can happen sometimes for ten days in a row. Tiredness gets to you – I can be pleasant to people when I'm in the studio, but I snap at the kids when I get home, and this leads to domestic pressure. It also gets to me when I have to do a lot of travelling. In the past year I've done over 25,000 miles. I worry when I'm stuck in a traffic jam, and I'm due at the gig.

When I stop playing after working every night for a long period, I feel ill. It's as though I get withdrawal symptoms.

When you're on the road, you just get into the swing of it. The tiredness hits you when you get home after the tour.

It's a stress when, if you've been working hard, you have to decide whether to turn gigs down to get a rest. You're worried that if you do turn gigs down, people won't ring again.

Travelling long distances alone at night really gets to me. I've often been in danger of falling asleep. Because of this I've had a CB radio fitted, and using this keeps me awake.

If it takes more than two hours to get to a gig, it's a strain, unless you're going somewhere special.

I hate having to drive a long way. It produces terrible tension. I don't like being late.

Travelling is hard work. It's not so much the travelling, it's having to play when you get there.

The feeling of isolation in a strange town, with only a suitcaseful of your personal belongings, particularly if you are not extremely close 'bosom buddies' with at least one of your fellow musicians, can, over a long period, do serious damage. It started me on a drink problem (now thankfully passed) and is one of the major factors in creating piss-artists and junkies: it's easier to cope with, you see, if you're slightly gassed all the time.

Work underload

The business of earning a living can be very unchallenging from a musical point of view. Much of the freelance popular musician's work involves 'bread-and-butter' gigs, for instance, working in orchestras accompanying summer shows or pantomimes, or in the dance bands of ocean-going liners. The work is seen as unstimulating and boring, since the music scores become familiar after a few nights, and a season usually lasts for about three months. Musicians frequently support themselves with this type of work, and play the sort of music they enjoy, often jazz or jazz-orientated music, in pubs or jazz clubs for very little remuneration. A typically bitter comment:

Most dull, routine, unfulfilling jobs are bad for people: for creative, skilled people, they can be like a cancer. Most bread-and-butter gigs consist of 'worthless' music, and as usual it's the most creative musicians who suffer most from doing them. This is compounded 100 per cent by the total lack of understanding of the public.

Job satisfaction

This was a source of stress mentioned by several musicians. The main reasons for lack of job satisfaction were playing in a band which was unable to realize its musical potential, and playing with musicians of a different ability level. Typical comments were as follows:

It's frustrating being in a band that has creative potential, but the band has to play bread-and-butter music to earn a living. In order to play music you enjoy, you may have to get a rehearsal band together, and pay for it from your bread-and-butter gig.

I enjoy every type of music. The only time I don't get job satisfaction is when I'm in a situation where I have to play with incompetent musicians.

I don't like playing with musicians who aren't good enough.

I feel tense leading a band when the members aren't compatible, due to either personality or ability.

Career development

Many musicians in our interview sample, often those involved in freelance commercial work, were concerned as much with career stability as with career development. As long as these musicians were working steadily and were earning a living wage, they were fairly content. As was highlighted in the section on performance anxiety, the musician is as ambitious for musical satisfaction as for fame and fortune.

A source of great stress was the fear of 'not getting enough gigs'. As in other areas of work at the present time, jobs are becoming increasingly scarce. When 'the phone doesn't ring and the gigs don't come in', the musician may feel that work is now being given to another musician who is considered to be a better player than himself, and this leads to feelings of self-doubt, anxiety and depression. The comments of musicians illustrate these points:

If you aren't getting a lot of gigs, you start wondering if you're good enough.

If people don't ring you to offer work, your ego and pride suffer, and this leads to depression.

When people don't ring, you think: is it because there's no work, or is it because I'm not good enough?

When you've progressed from playing ordinary dance band gigs to being able to play more complex music, if someone else gets a gig instead of you, you start thinking you're not good enough.

Other fears are allied to these. For instance, if a musician has regular work, as in a club residency, he wonders how long it will last. Again, there is the fear for the musician that there is no pension for him when he reaches what would be considered retiring age in other professions. Musicians' comments on these insecurities were as follows:

> If you do a residency, your name gets forgotten, and people don't ring you to give you gigs. On the other hand, you may be working in a club, and the management want a change of face to keep the public happy, so they boot you out. I used to work for Mecca, and they can move you around a lot from one ballroom to another. You also worry about physical damage. For instance, what if you hurt your fingers?

> As a musician, you can't afford to be ill – you've got to keep soldiering on. And often, you prolong an illness by doing this. There's no pension at the end of the job. If you're fired, you can't go to a tribunal.

> You can't afford to worry about the future. Your best years are your first years, and you have to fight your decline. Musicians don't provide for their old age. When you're freelance, every gig is a challenge because you don't know what you'll have to cope with.

> There's a fair amount of hatred of musicians by club owners, because they have to pay Musicians' Union rates.

> You have to keep practising, and as you get older, you're not bothered about improving, just keeping up your standard of playing. You worry that younger, better players are going to usurp your place.

A further problem is that when he has played a gig, a musician may have to wait for payment. A well-known recording session musician said:

> Sometimes you have to wait two or three months, and the people that you owe money to, like tax and VAT people, don't want to wait. If you dare to ring up about payment, you can get abuse, and you stand a good chance of being blacklisted. In no other business would this practice be allowed.

Jazz musicians frequently felt that their music did not receive the recognition, or the reward, that it deserved:

> As an adult with responsibilities towards my family to make some kind of income, I find it very frustrating that people of world-class calibre, on the wages side, get nowhere near their counterparts on the concert platform. You get Itzhak Perlman doing a concert and he'll pack the place out. Unfortunately, if you've got a name British jazz player doing a concert, I think he'd find it difficult to get the same audience. And often, the talents and abilities that jazz musicians have are used in musical situations that are far beneath their capabilities, and this causes tremendous resentment and frustration. It's like a major surgeon who has to work as a hospital porter – it's a similar situation. The guy knows he can do a lot better, but the opportunities aren't there.

A common theme discussed by rock musicians in the interview sample was the split between the ideals of musicians and those of record company, management and agency executives. One rock musician was of the opinion that: 'Musicians are basically harmless people, which is why they're such marvellous fodder for the record industry. You can screw a musician better than you can screw anybody.'

He continued by saying that:

> The state of the management/agency situation is scandalous. In my experience all but a tiny percentage of agents and managers are either hopeless, bent or both. It's a total fiasco in which the musician *again* bears the brunt, and which alienates him even further. In addition, robbery within these areas, and the record industry, is actually *legal*. How else can a musician feel but downtrodden?

Perhaps especially for rock and pop musicians, success and financial reward bring their own problems, which are compounded when, as happens all too often, the success suddenly disappears:

> Once you move up into what I call the inner circle of music, you meet new people, you meet new taxes, new accountants, new lawyers, new agents – you have to have these people, and there are all the stress factors that go on. And then, it's all right while you're relatively successful, but when things start going wrong and you move out of the inner circle, you've still got all the inner circle problems. The problems you created as you built up never go away. It's one of those professions where, whoever you're going to see, whether it's a bank manager, or to get a mortgage or HP, they always go 'Well, how much do you earn a week?' And you can't say. I don't know how much I've earned this week. Sometimes I get royalties, sometimes there's a week where I doubt if I earn a penny. Next week I might earn $35,000 – I don't know. I've just got a new mortgage recently, but I got that more or less because of *who* I am. But for the average musician, it can be a nightmare. When I was working in the clubs and round the Top Rank ballrooms, and things like that, I couldn't get a pound overdraft. They wouldn't give it to you; you're in the famous category that's a frightener!

A pop musician described what happened when his group, which had enjoyed a string of hit records, split up:

> I was lumbered with all these amazing mortgages and insurances that I was told to take out by accountants to keep my tax down. It's fine when the money's coming in, but when you leave, you suddenly find yourself stuck with these insurances and mortgages, and you've got to sell your home and move out.

There are thus stresses for the popular musician at all stages of career development.

Relationships at work

It was interesting to find that musicians tended to be somewhat cynical and wary regarding their fellows, and in fact, their observations were often of a scathingly critical nature. Criticisms tended to fall into two main areas, namely those relating to fellow musicians, and those relating to bandleaders and musical directors. Some comments by freelance commercial musicians regarding their colleagues were as follows:

As a race, musicians aren't very stable.

Musicians are a cynical bunch by nature.

Musicians can be two-faced.

One of a musician's greatest pastimes is stirring it and taking the piss.

The music business is a big piss-take. You've got to be able to take snide remarks.

Most musicians play to show off. They often have a misplaced idea of their own abilities. It often seems that the harder you work, the less you get. Wasters often seem to get farther. I always get my own gigs, do the arranging, and get the other musicians in the band. There's no correlation between money and effort at the end of the day. I'd like to be given gigs without so much organization involved. You have to make a compromise between the facade you show to other musicians and your inner self.

In the music business, you have to fit in: play golf, go to clubs frequented by musicians, and don't be too individualistic, honest, intense or serious about music.

Getting on in the music business is related less to your actual capabilities than to whether your face fits with people who matter.

When you're in a residency, it's the same old faces every night, and familiarity can breed contempt.

Typical comments about musical directors and bandleaders were as follows:

I get very annoyed by people who don't know what they're talking about, for instance some musical directors.

There are too many people in the music business, for instance, some musical directors, who are just posers and don't really know anything about music.

Bandleaders are a race apart. They've got to be because they're employers. They're more businessmen than musicians, and sometimes they're bad musicians. This can lead to bad feeling because musicians resent someone who isn't as good a player as themselves, and who is getting a lot more money.

For his part, one musical director had the following observation to make:

Musicians are selfish, greedy people with a lot of ego. They've given me a hard time. They're often fools to themselves: they drink to cover up anxiety, and then blame mistakes on the drink. I don't socialize with musicians.

The interview sample, therefore, provided evidence that the musician can be suspicious, wary and resentful of his colleagues and work superiors. These findings bear resemblances to those of Schulz (1981) and James (1984), who found that classical musicians have problems in relating to their fellow orchestra members and to conductors.

Relationships in the working situation also include those that the musician has with his audiences and with the music press. One well-known jazz musician made some pungent remarks on this subject:

> I resent critics and audiences who look down on you if you are not American. I have heard and worked with some diabolical American musicians, but because they come from the other side of the 'pond', they can do no wrong to these people. A British group to these people, *no matter how good*, just gets written off!
>
> Critics can dismiss a performer's life's work at literally a stroke. Any opinion can only be subjective and when the general public, by and large, are too dumb to find out for themselves about artists, this kind of power is very damaging.
>
> If you find a good critic kill him before he or she becomes bad!!

For the rock musician involved in the gruelling schedule of long tours abroad, contact with his colleagues can become a special ordeal. One musician summed this up as follows:

> Living together as a small group of people who are totally different characters, sleeping in the same hotel, eating, drinking together, you've got different views on life – you've got to live with them month after month, and it can be a nightmare.

A sense of unreality is often engendered in the relationship that the musician has with the people who appear on the periphery of the tour:

> If you're a pop group doing a tour, you never meet real people. You meet record company people and promotion people, you meet hotel staff, and if you do meet ordinary people in the guise of fans, they always assume they've got to present themselves as super-hip because they're meeting a pop group. They never meet you on an ordinary level. I ended up on the old Southern Comfort. You lose touch with reality. It throws you out of gear. You're not meeting people with ordinary problems. People talk to you about product, and points, and offshore banking deals.

Under the weight of these pressures, there is frequently only one way out – the break-up of the band:

One of the interesting things is that bands set out to achieve success, and yet success is usually the thing that breaks them up. It's that business of working with a very small group of people in a hot-house situation. There's that initial stage where everyone's going through the same thing, and then the splits start to occur. The band's doing okay, then one person in the band starts to become freakier and freakier. He's really hard to work with, or totally erratic, may not turn up, all that sort of thing. That can break the others, one real freako who's good, like he's the star guitar player or whatever, but the others just don't know if he's going to be there on Thursday night. That can really give someone stomach ulcers. I've seen this in a number of bands – that feeling of someone taking you where you just don't want to go.

Effects on social and family life

The musician's lifestyle has the effect of producing pressure on personal relationships. Pressures are caused because of the un-sociable hours that the musician often works, and because of the considerable amount of time he may spend away from home. The wife or partner rarely shares the musician's often consuming passion for his music, and often wishes for a more 'normal' lifestyle. As one musician commented:

> There's a difference in the time scale and the lifestyle of the ordinary person and the musician. It affects the social life of both myself and my wife, and it can make me feel disorientated.

Personality

During the interviews in the preliminary survey each musician was asked to complete the Eysenck Personality Questionnaire (Eysenck and Eysenck, 1975), since no previous personality studies of professional popular musicians existed.

The Eysenck Personality Questionnaire scores of the interview sample appear in Table 4.1. It was interesting to find that, in comparison with the overall mean male adult scores given in the manual of the EPQ, both the psychoticism and neuroticism scores for musicians were elevated. The musicians' mean neuroticism score was also higher than any of the mean neuroticism scores for various professional groups provided in the manual. This high level of neuroticism in the interview sample, if taken as a measure of anxiety, is comparable to the above-average levels of anxiety found in the sample of classical musicians by Kemp (1981). The interview sample also resembled the sample of professional artists studied by Gotz and Gotz (1979a,b), who also had elevated neuroticism and psychoticism scores. There is thus some evidence that popular

Table 4.1 *Ages and EPQ scores of 70 professional popular musicians*

	Age		Psychoticism		Extroversion		Neuroticism		Lie scale	
	Mean	SD	Mean	SD	Mean	SD	Mean	SD	Mean	SD
All males (N = 70)	40.00	9.31	4.06	2.12	12.40	4.32	12.74	5.52	7.70	3.75
Trumpeters (N = 10)	45.20	7.42	4.10	2.28	12.70	5.92	9.50	6.28	9.80	4.80
Trombonists (N = 6)	43.60	7.25	3.00	2.36	11.00	5.94	14.00	4.24	6.60	4.44
Saxophonists (N = 13)	43.00	10.51	3.70	2.13	12.70	3.35	12.00	4.99	8.60	3.12
Pianists (N = 11)	41.90	10.35	3.73	2.24	11.45	4.98	14.72	5.71	8.20	3.42
Guitarists (N = 10)	35.50	6.39	4.90	1.91	12.90	2.84	16.90	5.96	6.20	3.25
Bassists (N = 10)	37.30	7.80	4.20	2.09	11.50	4.45	10.50	4.52	6.00	3.05
Drummers (N = 10)	36.00	10.38	4.50	2.01	13.90	3.41	12.10	5.00	7.60	3.94

SD = standard deviation

musicians are similar in personality to classical musicians, and also to members of other creative professions. It may be that musicians are intrinsically more 'neurotic' than average, but alternatively one might conclude that the stresses of the musician's profession produce high levels of anxiety, and in this respect Humphrey (1977) states that neuroticism scores increase when the individual is experiencing stress.

Eysenck's psychoticism dimension measures traits of tough-mindedness and suspiciousness, and, considering the interview sample's comments regarding their fellow musicians, their overall elevated psychoticism scores are not altogether unexpected.

In looking at the scores of players of different instruments, trumpeters gained the lowest neuroticism scores. This is in accord with other studies, for instance that of Davies (1978). It is interesting to note that guitarists gained the highest score on both psychoticism and neuroticism. With such a small sample, it is difficult to draw conclusions as to why this should be.

Interview data: conclusions

The analysis of the interview data pinpointed the fact that a high percentage of the sample perceived several stressors to be sources of great pressure. Isolation of the stress of needing to reach self-imposed standards of musicianship highlighted the dilemma of the performing artist, and was in alignment with previous studies of musicians and stress. The findings from the Eysenck Personality Questionnaire survey also drew attention to the fact that the musician is subject to above-average levels of anxiety, and that he bears a resemblance to other 'creative' personalities.

The interview data, combined with information derived from a review of the literature, provided a rich source of information regarding stresses in popular music. This proved invaluable in terms of formulating the design for the main research survey.

5
What are popular musicians like?

The questionnaire

The main part of the survey into popular musicians and stress was concerned with the devising of a comprehensive questionnaire, and its subsequent distribution to a large sample of musicians. The analysis of the interview material, previously validated measures of stress, and information from previous research findings formed the basis for the questionnaire. The questionnaire is printed in full on pages 121–30 and the different sections of the questionnaire are described in detail here.

Job demographics
In order to compare and contrast as fully as possible the stressors and stress outcomes experienced by musicians working in different areas of popular music, questions were included concerning instruments played, types of music played, and types of setting in which musical activities took place.

With regard to instruments played, musicians were asked to name their main instrument, and also any other instrument played. Regarding types of music played, the authors composed a comprehensive list of different types of popular music, consisting of ten items. These were jazz; rock; pop; commercial/easy listening/middle-of-the-road music; dance-band music; jazz-funk/fusion/crossover music; disco-funk; reggae; soul/rhythm and blues; and folk. Musicians were asked to rate how frequently they played each type of music on a five-point Likert-type scale containing the dimensions 1 (never), 2 (rarely), 3 (sometimes), 4 (often), and 5 (mainly).

Relating to types of musical setting, it was apparent from the interview data that there are three main situations in which a popular musician works. These are: as a member of a gigging band; as a resident musician; and as a session musician. Again, musicians were asked to rate on a five-point Likert-type scale how often they played in each of these musical settings.

Personal demographics
To gain as clear a picture as possible of the popular musician, questions were included regarding whether the respondent worked

in a non-musical job immediately after leaving school, and at what age the respondent became a professional musician. Also, since a number of musicians in the preliminary interviews mentioned that they gave tuition on their instrument in order to supplement their income, respondents were asked to state whether they taught as well as played. Other items included were: age, marital status, number of children, educational qualifications, and salary.

Work stressor questionnaire
This questionnaire consisted of 53 items, the majority of which were derived from the analysis of the interview material, and also from previous research findings. The items were accompanied by a five-point Likert-type rating scale ranging from 'no pressure at all' (rating of 1) to 'a great deal of pressure' (rating of 5), and were grouped under the following broad sub-category headings: factors intrinsic to the job, career development, relationships at work, role in the organization, effects on social and family life, and perform-ance anxiety and related anxieties. Examples of items were: 'playing at a venue with bad conditions', 'doing a long tour', 'coping with an instrument that is physically difficult to play' and 'feeling tense or nervous when playing a live gig with your regular band'.

Coping ability
In order to measure the degree to which musicians adopted positive, stress-reducing coping strategies, items from the coping section of the Conflict/Stress Questionnaire by Steinmetz (1979) were used. The coping strategies, namely relaxation techniques, informal relaxation techniques, exercise, talk to someone you know, leave work area, and use humour, were scored on a five-point Likert-type scale from 1 (never) to 5 (always) in answer to the question: 'How often do you use the following measures to relax?'

Type A coronary-prone behaviour
Possibly the single most significant factor to be isolated by stress research has been the Type A coronary-prone behavioural syn-drome. Evidence for this stems from the work of the two cardiologists, Friedman and Rosenman (1974) who categorized individuals as having either Type A or Type B personalities. Type A behaviour is typified by a striving for high achievement, with a tendency to undertake several tasks concurrently, and the conse-quence that tasks are often not completed satisfactorily. There is a sense of time urgency, with a resultant programming of too much work into a limited period of time. Inappropriate aggression and hostility are further traits of the Type A personality, with tension of

the facial muscles and explosiveness of speech. On the other hand, Type B patterns involve passivity or not being overly ambitious, restraint and not being prone to developing stress-related disorders. Friedman and Rosenman believe that individuals with Type A personalities are predisposed to develop premature coronary heart disease.

It was felt that it would be helpful to include a measure of Type A behaviour in popular musicians and therefore an adapted version of the Bortner scale (1967) was included in the questionnaire. This scale was chosen, since it is one of the most widely validated and comprehensive of the Type A coronary-prone behaviour inventories. The authors' adapted scale consisted of 14 items, each with an 11-point rating scale. Included were items from Bortner's four sub-scale sections: hard-driving, job involvement, speed, impatience, and overall Type A behaviour. The scale yields scores from 14 to 154, the lowest scores being indicative of Type A behaviour.

Psychosomatic health

Physical and mental well-being were measured by the Gurin Psychosomatic Symptom List (Gurin et al., 1960). This is a validated self-completion measure of psychosomatic health, and was specifically modified by Marshall (1977) in her large-scale British study investigating the job pressures of male managers. This modified version was selected for inclusion in the survey questionnaire, and consisted of 20 items representing four sub-scales of psychosomatic health: psychological anxiety, physical health, immobilization and physical anxiety. The summation of all the scores also provided an overall psychosomatic health score.

Alcohol and cigarette consumption

Three question items were included in order to acquire details regarding musicians' alcohol and cigarette consumption. These items were adapted from those used in the Henley Executive Health Questionnaire (Cooper and Melhuish, 1980). Respondents were asked: 'Over the past year, which of the following best describes your drinking habits? (one drink is a single whisky, gin or brandy, a glass of wine, sherry or port, or half a pint of beer)'. Drinking habit categorizations ranged through teetotal, an occasional drink, several drinks a week but not every day, regularly 1 or 2 drinks a day, and regularly, 3–6 drinks a day.

Regarding cigarette consumption, musicians were asked to state whether they had never smoked regularly, had given up smoking, or were currently smoking. Those who were currently smoking were asked to state the average number of cigarettes smoked per day, selecting from seven quantity categories ranging from 0–5 per day to 40 plus per day.

Use of illegal drugs
The use of illegal drugs by popular musicians is a subject which creates interest in the media. Since no previous statistics existed regarding British popular musicians, a section on illegal drugs was, therefore, included. Musicians were asked: 'How often, if ever, do you use the following drugs? Your answers will remain anonymous and strictly confidential, and are for statistical analysis only.' Respondents were asked to rate, using a five-point Likert-type scale with the categories never, rarely, sometimes, often, and a lot, use of the following drugs: cannabis, LSD, amphetamines, cocaine and heroin.

Job satisfaction
Job satisfaction was measured by using two items, slightly modified, and taken from the Job Satisfaction Scale used in numerous stress research studies (for example, Caplan et al., 1975; Cooper and Melhuish, 1980). Musicians were requested to indicate how much they agreed with the statements 'I feel fairly well satisfied with my present gig(s)' and 'I find real enjoyment in my work as a musician', using a five-point Likert-type scale from 1 (strongly agree) to 5 (strongly disagree).

Data collection from the main sample of popular musicians

As large a number as possible of professional musicians, working in all areas of popular music, was needed for the study, and it was decided that the best way to contact them was by the use of Musicians' Union directories, since these contain the names and addresses of all musicians who are union members in the British Isles.

The London Musicians' Union Directory formed the main focus for the selection of popular musicians, since London is the entertainment capital of Great Britain. The authors chose the names of all musicians who were known by them to be professional popular musicians. All areas of popular music were covered, and the musicians ranged from the very eminent to the not-so-eminent. In all, 800 names were selected, and of these, only 30 were female. This is a regrettably small figure, but these were the only names known to the authors, and were an indication that popular music is a male-dominated profession. Nevertheless, it was hoped that enough information would be provided to compare and contrast stresses experienced by male and female musicians.

The 800 questionnaires were distributed by post and a total of 246 completed questionnaires were returned. One problem which must be borne in mind is that musicians are a mobile population, and tend to change their addresses quite frequently. Taking this fact into account, it was felt that the response rate was good for a postal questionnaire survey of this nature.

Breakdown of the survey sample into sub-categories

The aim of the survey was twofold: (1) to isolate the stressors and stress outcomes experienced by professional popular musicians as a whole, and (2) to compare and contrast the stressors and stress outcomes experienced by musicians working in different areas of popular music. Therefore, in order to fulfil the latter aim, it was necessary to utilize a method whereby the survey sample could be broken down into sub-categories of different types of music played and different musical settings.

Ten types of 'music played' were included in the questionnaire. These were: jazz, rock, pop, commercial, dance-band music, jazz-funk, disco-funk, reggae, soul, and folk. For purposes of analysis, the categories jazz and jazz-funk were subsumed under the heading 'jazz', the categories rock, pop, disco-funk, reggae, soul and folk under the heading 'pop', and the categories commercial and dance band music under the heading 'commercial'. Depending on which type of music was played most, therefore (as rated on the Likert-type scale from 1, never, to 5, mainly), a musician was designated as being either a jazz musician, a pop musician, or a commercial musician.

With regard to musical setting, three categories were included in the questionnaire. These were: (1) member of gigging band, (2) resident musician and (3) session musician. Thus, if a musician stated that he worked mainly in category one he was designated a gig musician, if in category two he was designated a resident musician, and if in category three, he was designated a session musician.

A method of combining type of music played and type of musical setting played in was needed, in order to ascertain how many musicians worked as jazz gig musicians, how many worked as pop gig musicians, how many worked as commercial session musicians, and so forth. Therefore, a 3 by 3 contingency table was designed.

Table 5.1 shows the breakdown of musicians into the separate music played/musical setting categories. It was found that no musicians fitted into the jazz/session musician, jazz/resident musician or pop/resident musician categories and therefore the final breakdown of the survey sample was into six sub-categories: (1) jazz/gig

Table 5.1   *Number of musicians assigned to different music played/musical setting categories*

	Jazz musician	Pop musician	Commercial musician
Gig musician	64	62	20
Session musician	0	44	38
Resident musician	0	0	18

musicians, (2) pop/gig musicians, (3) commercial/gig musicians, (4) pop/session musicians, (5) commercial/session musicians, and (6) commercial/resident musicians. These formed the comparison groups for the survey.

The main sample of popular musicians

Table 5.2 illustrates the personal demographic details of the main sample of popular musicians. A total of 232 male popular musicians and 14 female popular musicians returned completed questionnaires.

Age
It is interesting to note that 60.3 per cent of the sample were aged under forty years, an indication that popular music tends to be a young person's profession. More than a quarter of the sample (27 per cent) were single, and of the respondents between the ages twenty and twenty-nine, 77.8 per cent were unmarried. Relating to this, with regard to number of children, a high percentage of respondents (39.2 per cent) had no children.

Marital status
Only 12.5 per cent of the sample as a whole were separated or divorced. This figure appears to be quite low when compared to national norms. Overall, one marriage in four ends in divorce within fifteen years in Britain (*Social Trends*, 1983). The highest number of those separated or divorced fell within the age ranges forty to fifty-nine years. For respondents aged forty to forty-nine, the figure was 19.2 per cent, while for those aged fifty to fifty-nine, it was 18.4 per cent.

Education
Turning to educational attainment, compared to the British population norms provided by *Social Trends* (1986), musicians generally appear to be slightly less well educated. Only 30.6 per cent had

Table 5.2 *Personal demographics of main sample of popular musicians*

	% (no.)			% (no.)	
Sex			*Number of children*		
Male		(232)	None	39.2	(95)
Female		(14)	One	23.8	(59)
			Two	23.8	(59)
Age			Three	9.6	(23)
Under 20 years	0.8	(2)	Four or more	3.6	(10)
20–29 years	18.6	(47)			
30–39 years	40.9	(101)			
40–49 years	21.9	(53)	*Educational attainment*		
50–59 years	15.7	(38)	None	29.3	(72)
60–69 years	2.1	(5)	GCE 'O' Level/CSE	30.6	(75)
			'A' Level/Ordinary	13.6	(34)
Marital status			National Diploma		
Single	27.0	(66)	Higher National Diploma	1.2	(3)
Married	59.8	(145)	Music degree or diploma	12.8	(31)
Separated	4.6	(12)	Other university degree	9.9	(25)
Divorced	7.9	(20)	M.A./M.Sc.	2.1	(5)
Widowed	0.7	(3)	Ph.D.	0.5	(1)

attained 'O' level standard compared to 41 per cent of the British population, and only 13.6 per cent had attained 'A' level standard as opposed to 29 per cent in the population as a whole. On the other hand, musicians were comparable to the population in terms of possessing a university degree. The figures here were 9.9 per cent for musicians, and 9 per cent for the population as a whole. Interestingly, only 12.8 per cent of the survey sample possessed a music degree or diploma, pointing to the fact that a music degree is not a necessity for a career in popular music. In terms of education as a whole, there was a strong trend for younger musicians to have higher educational attainment, and this follows the pattern of population norms.

Job details

The job details of the main sample of popular musicians are presented in Table 5.3. There was a fairly even breakdown of musicians into sub-categories, with 64 jazz musicians, 106 pop musicians (62 pop/gig musicians and 44 pop/session musicians), and 76 commercial musicians (20 commercial/gig musicians, 38 commercial/session musicians and 18 commercial/resident musicians). There was also a fairly even breakdown in terms of main instrument, with 30 brass players (16 trumpeters and 14 trombonists), 31 reed players (27

Table 5.3 *Job demographics of main sample of popular musicians*

	Male	Female
Music played/musical setting		
Jazz/gig	60	4
Pop/gig	59	3
Commercial/gig	17	3
Pop/session	40	4
Commercial/session	38	0
Commercial/residency	18	0

	% (no.)			% (no.)	
Main instrument			*Type of non-musical job*		
Trumpet	6.5	(16)	*on leaving school*		
Trombone	5.7	(14)	Manual	23.2	(59)
Saxophone	11.0	(27)	Non-manual	43.9	(106)
Flute	0.8	(2)	No job	32.9	(81)
Clarinet	0.8	(2)			
Piano	9.3	(23)			
Keyboards	6.1	(15)	*Annual salary*		
Guitar	15.0	(37)	Under £4,000	14.5	(35)
Bass	15.4	(38)	£4,000–6,000	14.5	(35)
Drums	19.1	(47)	£6,000–8,000	12.8	(31)
Percussion	1.2	(3)	£8,000–10,000	10.7	(26)
Harmonica	0.4	(1)	£10,000–12,000	9.9	(24)
Vocals	5.3	(13)	£12,000–14,000	6.6	(16)
Bandleader	0.8	(2)	£14,000–16,000	5.8	(14)
Arranger	1.2	(3)	£16,000–18,000	3.3	(8)
Violin	1.2	(3)	£18,000–20,000	3.3	(8)
			Over £20,000	18.6	(49)
Age turned professional					
16–20 years	59.2	(142)	*Teach music*		
21–25 years	33.4	(86)	Yes	35.0	(86)
26–30	5.4	(13)	No	65.0	(160)
31–35	0.8	(2)			
36–40	0.4	(1)			
41–45	0.4	(1)	*Other current job*		
46–50	0.0	(0)	Yes	4.9	(12)
51–55	0.4	(1)	No	95.1	(234)
Worked in non-musical job			*Type of other current job*		
on leaving school			Manual	1.2	(3)
Yes	67.1	(165)	Non-manual	3.7	(9)
No	32.9	(81)	No other job	95.1	(234)

saxophonists, 2 flautists and 2 clarinettists), 38 piano and keyboard players, 37 guitarists, 38 bassists and 47 drummers. It would thus appear that the main sample are a fairly representative cross-section of popular musicians as a whole.

Age turned professional

The profession of popular music, like other performing arts or 'show business' professions, i , not a conventional or 'safe' one, and this is illustrated by the fact that a minority of respondents became professional musicians either immediately on leaving school or on completing a music college course. As was stated earlier, only 12.8 per cent of respondents possessed a music degree. The majority of musicians (67.1 per cent) worked in a non-musical job on leaving school, and although the majority (59.2 per cent) had become professional by the age of twenty years, the specific age at which most musicians became professional was twenty-one, with 14.2 per cent 'turning pro' at this age. This suggests that musicians decided, or were persuaded by their parents, to initially gain some conventional work experience. Having in some cases worked through apprenticeships or gained other qualifications, and having reached the 'age of consent', they weighed up the odds, took a calculated risk, and decided to become professional musicians. A small number (2 per cent) did not feel ready to make this move until after the age of thirty, with one respondent not becoming professional until the age of fifty-three. This points to the fact that it is felt that there is an element of risk in becoming a professional musician, with the consequent stressful worry regarding whether one will be successful, having given up a conventional job.

With regard to type of job worked in prior to becoming professional, 43.9 per cent of respondents worked in non-manual jobs, while 23.2 per cent were involved in manual work. A wide spectrum of jobs was covered including librarian, engineer, teacher, farm labourer, factory worker, plumber, hairdresser and civil servant.

Annual salary

In considering annual salary, it would appear that the main sample are similar to national norms. According to *Social Trends* (1986), the average gross annual salary of British male employees in 1984 was £9,300 (£178.8 per week). 52.5 per cent of the survey sample earned less than £10,000 per year, while 47.5 per cent earned more than £10,000. Of the highest earners (those earning over £20,000 annually), the highest percentage (38.6 per cent) were in the age range thirty to thirty-nine. Interestingly, there appeared to be an inverse relationship between educational attainment and high earnings. Of those earning over £20,000 annually, 29.5 per cent had no

Table 5.4   *Personal demographics of sub-categories of popular musicians*

	Jazz/gig % (no.)		Pop/gig % (no.)		Commercial/ gig % (no.)		Pop/session % (no.)		Commercial/ session % (no.)		Commercial/ residency % (no.)	
Age												
Under 20 years	1.6	(1)	1.7	(1)								
20–29 years	9.4	(6)	35.0	(21)	20.0	(4)	18.6	(8)	8.1	(3)	16.7	(3)
30–39 years	35.9	(23)	51.7	(31)	30.0	(6)	55.8	(24)	18.9	(7)	44.4	(8)
40–49 years	28.1	(18)	11.6	(7)	35.0	(7)	20.9	(9)	24.3	(9)	16.7	(3)
50–59 years	21.9	(14)			15.0	(3)	4.7	(2)	43.2	(16)	16.7	(3)
60–69 years	3.1	(2)							5.5	(2)	5.5	(1)
Marital status												
Single	20.3	(13)	41.7	(25)	20.0	(4)	31.0	(13)	10.8	(4)	33.3	(6)
Married	68.8	(44)	48.3	(29)	65.0	(13)	52.4	(22)	73.0	(27)	50.0	(9)
Separated	3.1	(2)	5.0	(3)	5.0	(1)	4.8	(2)	2.7	(1)	11.1	(2)
Divorced									10.8	(4)		
Widowed	7.8	(5)	5.0	(3)	10.0	(2)	11.8	(5)	2.7	(1)	5.6	(1)
Number of children												
None	39.7	(25)	51.7	(31)	25.0	(5)	41.9	(18)	19.4	(7)	44.4	(8)
One	17.5	(11)	16.7	(10)	25.0	(5)	30.2	(13)	27.8	(10)	44.4	(8)
Two	23.8	(15)	23.3	(14)	40.0	(8)	18.6	(8)	27.8	(10)	11.2	(2)
Three	14.3	(9)	5.0	(3)	10.0	(2)	7.0	(3)	16.7	(6)		
Four or more	4.7	(3)	3.3	(2)			2.3	(1)	8.3	(3)		

Table 5.4 *continued*
Personal demographics of sub-categories of popular musicians

	Jazz/gig % (no.)		Pop/gig % (no.)		Commercial/gig % (no.)		Pop/session % (no.)		Commercial/session % (no.)		Commercial/residency % (no.)	
Educational attainment												
None	23.4	(15)	23.3	(14)	30.0	(6)	27.9	(12)	48.6	(18)	33.3	(6)
GCE 'O' Level/CSE	32.8	(21)	36.7	(22)	25.0	(5)	30.2	(13)	24.4	(9)	22.2	(4)
'A' Level/Ordinary National Diploma	12.5	(8)	15.0	(9)	10.0	(2)	16.3	(7)	13.5	(5)	11.1	(2)
Higher National Diploma			1.7	(1)							11.1	(2)
Music degree or diploma	10.9	(7)	10.0	(6)	15.0	(3)	16.3	(7)	13.5	(5)	16.7	(3)
Other university degree	15.6	(10)	11.7	(7)	15.0	(3)	7.0	(3)			5.6	(1)
M.A./M.Sc.	3.1	(2)	1.6	(1)	5.0	(1)	2.3	(1)				
Ph.D.	1.6	(1)										

educational qualifications, while a further 29.5 per cent had only attained 'O' level standard.

A number of respondents supplemented their income by non-playing methods. 35 per cent of the survey sample taught as well as played music, while 4.9 per cent stated that they had another current job. Of these, 3.7 per cent worked part-time in music shops. There is thus evidence that it is not always possible to earn a living purely from playing music.

Sub-categories of popular musicians

Age
There was a significant difference in the ages of the sub-groups of musicians (Kruskal Wallis One-Way Analysis of Variance, $p < 0.000$), with pop/gig musicians being the youngest, and commercial/session musicians being the oldest. Pop musicians overall formed the youngest grouping, with 88.4 per cent of pop/gig musicians and 74.4 per cent of pop/session musicians being under the age of forty. This is to be expected, considering the 'youthful' image of pop music. On the other hand, the largest percentage (43.2 per cent) of commercial/session musicians was in the age range fifty to fifty-nine years. (See Table 5.4.)

Marital status
Although not statistically significant, there was a similar contrast between pop/gig musicians and commercial/session musicians with regard to marital status. Pop/gig musicians represented the highest percentage (41.7 per cent) of single respondents, while commercial/session musicians represented the highest percentage (73 per cent) of married respondents. Commercial/session musicians also had the highest number of children, with 16.7 per cent having three or more, while pop/gig musicians represented the highest percentage (51.7 per cent) with no children.

Education
A similarly striking contrast was observed with regard to educational attainment. Commercial/session musicians were the least educationally qualified, with 48.6 per cent having no educational attainment, while pop/gig musicians represented the lowest percentage (23.3 per cent) with no educational qualification.

Therefore, from an observation of personal demographic details, the most interesting factor to emerge is that pop/gig musicians and commercial/session musicians present as two very disparate groups, based on a significant difference in age. Commercial/session musicians were older, more frequently married, had more children, and were the least educationally qualified.

Job details
Table 5.5 presents the job details of the sub-categories of popular musicians. With regard to main instrument, there were no brass players among pop/gig musicians, unlike other sub-groups. There was a preponderance of guitarists among pop/gig musicians (30.6 per cent), closely followed by drummers (27.4 per cent). There is thus an indication that pop music still tends to be dominated by the guitar.

Age turned professional
Commercial/session musicians represented the highest percentage of respondents (75.3 per cent) to have turned professional by the age of twenty years. On the other hand, jazz/gig musicians showed the greatest tendency to become professional at a later age, with 3.9 per cent turning professional between the ages of twenty-six and thirty and 3.2 per cent between the ages of thirty-one and thirty-five. One jazz/gig musician did not turn professional until the age of fifty-three. There is a suggestion of a greater reticence on the part of musicians to commit themselves full-time to jazz than to other types of music, reflecting the fact that jazz is not a generally viable commercial proposition.

Annual salary
There was a significant difference ($p < 0.000$) in the annual salaries earned by different sub-groups of musicians, with commercial/session musicians representing the highest-paid group. 46.0 per cent of these respondents earned over £20,000 annually. They were closely followed by pop/session musicians, 30.1 per cent of whom earned over £20,000 annually. Therefore, overall, session musicians are the highest earners in the world of popular music. Although it may be possible to make a fortune as a member of a pop group, only 14.5 per cent of pop/gig musicians earned over £20,000 annually. Commercial/gig musicians emerged as the least well-paid of the six groups, with 80 per cent earning less than £10,000 annually.

Jazz/gig musicians represented the highest percentage (59.4 per cent) of respondents who taught music as well as played. More jazz/gig musicians taught than did not teach, whereas the reverse was true for other musicians. Jazz/gig musicians were also the group most frequently, at 12.5 per cent, to have another job. There is thus

Table 5.5   *Job demographics of sub-categories of popular musicians*

	Jazz/gig % (no.)	Pop/gig % (no.)	Commercial/ gig % (no.)	Pop/session % (no.)	Commercial/ session % (no.)	Commercial/ residency % (no.)
Main instrument						
Trumpet	12.5 (8)		5.0 (1)	2.3 (1)	15.8 (6)	11.1 (2)
Trombone	9.4 (6)				15.8 (6)	5.6 (1)
Saxophone	20.3 (13)	4.8 (3)	5.0 (1)	11.4 (5)	10.5 (4)	
Flute				2.3 (1)	2.6 (1)	
Clarinet	1.6 (1)	4.8 (3)	10.0 (2)	6.8 (3)	2.6 (1)	16.5 (3)
Piano	10.9 (7)	8.1 (5)	10.0 (2)	15.9 (7)	13.2 (5)	5.6 (1)
Keyboards		30.6 (19)	15.0 (3)	13.6 (6)		5.6 (1)
Guitar	7.8 (5)	16.1 (10)	20.0 (4)	13.6 (6)	7.9 (3)	27.8 (5)
Bass	14.1 (9)	27.4 (17)	15.0 (3)	22.7 (10)	10.5 (4)	27.8 (5)
Drums	14.1 (9)		15.0 (3)		7.9 (3)	
Percussion	1.6 (1)			2.3 (1)	2.6 (1)	
Harmonica		0.4 (1)				
Vocals	1.6 (1)	6.6 (4)	15.0 (3)	6.8 (3)	5.4 (2)	
Bandleader			5.0 (1)		2.6 (1)	
Arranger	1.6 (1)				2.6 (1)	
Violin	4.5 (3)			2.3 (1)		
Annual salary						
Under £4,000	22.6 (14)	16.1 (10)	25.0 (5)	11.6 (5)	8.1 (3)	5.6 (1)
£4,000–6,000	17.7 (11)	19.4 (12)	5.0 (1)	7.0 (3)	8.1 (3)	27.8 (5)
£6,000–8,000	12.9 (8)	8.1 (5)	40.0 (8)	4.7 (2)		27.8 (5)
£8,000–10,000	21.0 (13)	12.9 (8)	10.0 (2)		2.7 (1)	11.1 (2)
£10,000–12,000	9.7 (6)	14.5 (9)	5.0 (1)	7.0 (3)	8.1 (3)	11.1 (2)
£12,000–14,000	1.6 (1)	3.2 (2)	5.0 (1)	9.3 (4)	13.5 (5)	16.6 (3)

Table 5.5 continued
Job demographics of sub-categories of popular musicians

	Jazz/gig % (no.)		Pop/gig % (no.)		Commercial/ gig % (no.)		Pop/session % (no.)		Commercial/ session % (no.)		Commercial/ residency % (no.)	
£14,000–16,000	3.2	(2)	6.5	(4)			18.6	(8)	2.7	(1)		
£16,000–18,000	1.6	(1)	4.8	(3)	5.0	(1)	4.7	(2)	10.8	(4)		
£18,000–20,000	1.6	(1)					7.0	(3)				
Over £20,000	8.1	(5)	14.5	(9)	5.0	(1)	30.1	(13)	46.0	(17)		
Teach music												
Yes	59.4	(38)	25.0	(15)	35.0	(7)	18.6	(8)	31.6	(12)	35.3	(6)
No	40.6	(26)	75.0	(45)	65.0	(13)	81.4	(35)	68.4	(26)	64.7	(11)
Other current job												
Yes	12.5	(8)	1.6	(1)	5.0	(1)	2.3	(1)	2.6	(1)	100.0	(18)
No	87.5	(56)	98.4	(61)	95.0	(19)	97.7	(43)	97.4	(37)		
Type of other current job												
Manual	3.0	(2)	1.6	(1)								
Non-manual	9.5	(6)			5.0	(1)	2.3	(1)	2.6	(1)		
No other job	87.5	(56)	98.4	(61)	95.0	(19)	97.7	(43)	97.4	(37)	100.0	(18)
Age turned professional												
16–20 years	51.8	(28)	63.9	(37)	65.0	(13)	63.9	(27)	75.3	(27)	44.5	(8)
21–25 years	39.1	(25)	36.1	(21)	20.0	(4)	30.2	(13)	24.3	(9)	44.5	(8)
26–30 years	3.9	(5)			15.0	(3)	6.9	(3)			11.0	(2)
31–35 years	3.2	(2)										

Table 5.5   *continued*
Job demographics of sub-categories of popular musicians

	Jazz/gig % (no.)	Pop/gig % (no.)	Commercial/ gig % (no.)	Pop/session % (no.)	Commercial/ session % (no.)	Commercial/ residency % (no.)
36–40 years	1.6 (1)				0.4 (1)	
41–45 years						
46–50 years						
51–55 years	0.4 (1)					
Worked in non-musical job on leaving school						
Yes	71.4 (45)	71.2 (42)	75.0 (15)	61.9 (26)	64.9 (24)	72.2 (13)
No	28.6 (18)	28.8 (17)	25.0 (5)	38.1 (16)	35.1 (12)	27.8 (5)
Type of non-musical job on leaving school						
Manual	14.3 (9)	32.2 (19)	35.0 (7)	20.5 (8)	27.0 (10)	23.2 (4)
Non-manual	57.1 (36)	39.0 (22)	40.0 (8)	41.4 (15)	37.9 (14)	49.0 (9)
No job	28.6 (18)	28.8 (17)	25.0 (5)	38.1 (16)	35.1 (12)	27.8 (5)

the impression that jazz musicians feel the greatest need to supplement their income from playing by other means.

The sample: summary

In comparing the different sub-categories of popular musicians, the commercial/session musician emerges with perhaps the most distinctive profile. He is the least well educated, turns professional youngest, is the most frequently married with the highest number of children, is older and is the highest earner. The pop/gig musician is at the other end of the spectrum, in terms of being the youngest, the least married, and with the fewest children.

The jazz/gig musician also has a fairly distinctive profile. He is the best educated in terms of higher educational qualifications, tends to turn professional later in life, teaches music more frequently, and also supports himself with another job more frequently.

Overall, session musicians represent the highest-paid group, while the commercial/gig musician emerges as the 'poor relation', being the least well-paid of all six groups.

6
What causes popular musicians stress and how do they cope?

High stressors

The main fact that emerged from an observation of the stressor variables in the questionnaire was that popular musicians overall perceived themselves to be highly stressed. Every stressor item was rated as being highly stressful by a percentage of the musicians in terms of being rated 4 or 5 on the five-point rating scale. Table 6.1 presents high stressors in rank order, as rated by the main sample.

Table 6.1 *Main sample: High stressors (scores 4 or 5) in rank order*

Stressor	% (no.)	
Feeling that you must reach or maintain the standards of musicianship that you set for yourself	51.3	(126)
Instruments or equipment not working properly	44.8	(110)
Having to read and play a difficult part at a recording session or gig	41.8	(103)
Worrying because of lack of gigs	38.6	(95)
Playing when there is inadequate rehearsal or preparation	38.2	(94)
Effects of noise when the music is heavily amplified	37.4	(92)
Endangering your life by having to drive a long distance after a gig when you are tired	33.3	(82)
Finding it difficult to get a good recording or management deal for your band or musical project	32.1	(79)
Having to sack a musician if you are a bandleader	30.5	(75)
Stress put upon personal relationships, e.g. marriage	30.5	(75)
Having to play after travelling a long distance	30.1	(74)
Feeling that you need to become better known and/or better paid	28.9	(71)
As an artist, coming into conflict with recording, management or agency executives who are involved in your career and who do not share your musical ideals	28.5	(70)
Doing recording sessions or rehearsals during the day, then having to do a gig at night	28.5	(70)
Waiting around for long periods at the gig before it's time to play	27.6	(68)
Waiting for payment to come through from a gig or session	27.2	(67)
Getting musicians to deputize at short notice	27.2	(67)
Having to play music you don't like, in order to earn a living	26.4	(65)

Table 6.1 *continued*

Stressor	%	(no.)
Doing an audition	24.4	(60)
Playing at a venue with bad conditions	23.5	(58)
Feeling lonely or bored in strange towns or hotels when on tour	23.2	(57)
Doing a long tour	23.1	(57)
Feeling tense or nervous when playing in the recording studio as a session musician	22.8	(56)
Having to work when work is available, making it difficult to take holidays	22.7	(56)
Worrying about all the musicians getting to the gig on time	22.0	(54)
Worrying about the lack of pensions and benefits in the music profession	22.0	(54)
Coping with an instrument that is physically difficult to play	21.5	(53)
Feeling tense or nervous when playing a live gig as a session musician	21.5	(53)
Worrying that your ability to play will leave you	20.4	(50)
Feeling that your musical ability is not appreciated because of the public's ignorance about music	20.3	(50)
Expensiveness of instruments and other musical equipment	19.5	(48)
If you are a member of a famous band, feeling that this puts special pressures on you	19.5	(48)
In the recording studio, disagreeing with your producer or engineer	19.5	(48)
Feeling that playing is only one part of being a musician	19.5	(48)
Working in the enclosed and isolated environment of the studio	19.1	(47)
Personality clashes with, or jealousy of other musicians	19.1	(47)
Coping with a bandleader or musical director whose musical ideas clash with yours	18.3	(45)
Having to do a routine, repetitive gig	17.1	(42)
Working at night, often into the early hours	15.5	(38)
Feeling tense or nervous when playing a live gig with your regular band	15.5	(38)
Feeling 'high' after a gig and having to unwind, often with the use of alcohol or drugs	14.6	(36)
Feeling tense or nervous when playing in the recording studio with your regular band	13.9	(34)
Keeping up with new equipment and technology	11.4	(28)
Having to mingle socially with other musicians so that you will keep getting gigs	11.0	(27)
Feeling alienated from people who lead a 'normal, everyday' lifestyle and who may regard you as a 'second-class citizen'	11.0	(27)
Worrying that your style of playing is no longer fashionable	11.0	(27)
Feeling that decisions about your band's musical policy are taken without consulting you	10.2	(25)
Worrying about the prospect of flying when you have a gig or tour in a foreign country	10.2	(25)

Table 6.1   *continued*

Stressor	% (no.)	
Coping with criticisms in the music press or from other musicians	10.1	(25)
Working alone, composing or arranging	9.8	(24)
Feeling that if you are too intense or honest about your music, other musicians will regard you with suspicion	8.9	(22)
Worrying about being sacked from a gig or band	4.4	(11)
Feeling that you have reached the top too soon	3.2	(8)

Factors intrinsic to the job
It was apparent that factors intrinsic to the job produced the highest source of pressure overall. The popular musician's overriding concern is with his playing, his performance, and the situation and circumstances of his performance.

Performance anxiety and related anxieties   The greatest pressure experienced by popular musicians was a performance-related anxiety, namely, 'feeling that you must reach or maintain the standards of musicianship that you set for yourself'. A high percentage, 51.3 per cent, rated this as a high stressor. One is thus drawn to the conclusion that the popular musician is a single-minded individual, driven towards the goal of artistic self-satisfaction, and pressure is, therefore, internally as well as externally imposed.

In terms of actual playing situations, working as a session musician was felt to be more stressful than working with one's regular band. This is probably related to the high degree of concentration required, and there is a 'work overload' factor incorporated here. 22.8 per cent of respondents found that 'feeling tense or nervous when playing in the recording studio as a session musician' was highly stressful, while 21.5 per cent rated doing a 'live gig' as a session musician a high stressor.

Interestingly, a relatively small percentage of musicians experienced a high degree of performance anxiety when working with their regular band. 15.5 per cent of respondents rated doing a live gig with their regular band as being highly stressful, while 13.9 per cent rated doing a recording session with their regular band as a source of high pressure. It is likely that being familiar with the playing of one's colleagues, and having the opportunity to rehearse material, serves to reduce stress, and this relates to the point made by Wilson (1985) regarding the degree of task mastery that has been attained. It appears that performance anxiety is perhaps somewhat less of a problem for the popular musician than for his classical colleague, as reported by, for instance, Schulz (1981).

Instruments and equipment 'Instruments or equipment not working properly' was reported by musicians as being the second greatest source of high pressure. 44.8 per cent rated this as a high stressor. Obviously the musician cannot give of his best if his instrument or equipment fails, and even the most highly organized musician suffers from broken guitar strings, malfunctioning mouthpieces, amplifiers breaking down, and so forth. This is therefore an ongoing source of tension.

21.5 per cent of the sample reported that 'coping with an instrument that is physically difficult to play' was a source of high pressure. Although not appearing to be quite as severe a problem as it is for classical musicians (for example, Schulz, 1981), this is nevertheless quite a high percentage. 19.5 per cent of the sample stated that 'the expensiveness of instruments and other musical equipment' was a high stressor, and this is not surprising when one considers that the cost of an individual's equipment can run into thousands of pounds. 'Keeping up with new equipment and technology' was a high stressor for only 11.4 per cent of the sample.

Work overload Work overload factors represented the largest block of high stressors for the popular musician, with four of these stressors being rated 'high' by more than 25 per cent of respondents. Again, there was the impression that the musician was distressed by any problem which prevented him from giving his best performance. The highest work overload stressor was 'having to read and play a difficult part at a recording session or gig'. This was the third highest stressor overall, and was reported by 41.8 per cent of respondents. There is a connection here with the high performance anxiety of working as a session musician: the demand for accurate rendition of a difficult piece of music, where failure will lead to loss of face with one's colleagues, and loss of money for the recording studio or musical organization.

'Playing when there is inadequate rehearsal or preparation' was rated as a high stressor by 38.2 per cent of respondents, and once more this was a pressure causing direct detriment to performance. Four other high overload stressors were directly related to fatigue. These were 'having to play after travelling a long distance' (30.1 per cent), 'doing recording sessions or rehearsals during the day, then having to do a gig at night' (28.5 per cent), 'doing a long tour' (23.1 per cent), and 'having to work when work is available, making it difficult to take holidays' (22.7 per cent).

Physical danger An aspect of physical danger, 'effects of noise when the music is heavily amplified', was rated as the sixth highest stressor overall. 37.4 per cent of respondents felt that this was a high stressor. Thus, the risks connected with high volume are recognized by a large proportion of popular musicians. Also, 'endangering your life by having to drive a long distance after a gig when you are tired' was felt to be a high stressor by a considerable number of respondents, 33.3 per cent in all.

Work underload   One of the main aspects of the popular musician's lifestyle is that he is subjected to periods of high pressure, alternating with periods of boredom, and this is frequently outside his control. When on tour, the musician must kill time in strange towns; he is often called upon to arrive at his appointed venue early to set up his equipment, although he may not be playing until much later in the evening. Bearing this in mind, 27.6 per cent of respondents felt that 'waiting around for long periods at the gig before it's time to play' was a source of high pressure, while 23.2 per cent regarded 'feeling lonely or bored in strange towns or hotels while on tour' as highly stressful. A further source of boredom is 'having to do a routine, repetitive gig', and this was very stressful for 17.1 per cent of respondents.

Job satisfaction   26.4 per cent of respondents felt that 'having to play music you don't like, in order to earn a living' was a high stressor. Therefore, more than a quarter of the main sample were in agreement with the findings of the study by Becker (1963).

Poor physical working conditions   Although not quite as stressful as for classical musicians, as evidenced for instance by the study of Schulz (1981), 'playing at a venue with bad conditions' was found to be a high stressor by quite a large number of popular musicians, 23.5 per cent in all.

'Working in the enclosed and isolated environment of the recording studio' was highly stressful for only 19.1 per cent of respondents. The main stress factors in the studio appear to be related to the work overload factor of concentration, rather than to the environment in itself.

Shift work   Shift work was rated as a high stressor by a relatively small percentage of respondents. 15.5 per cent of the main sample rated 'working at night, often into the early hours' as highly stressful. The majority of musicians appear to accept this factor as an intrinsic part of their job, and adjust accordingly.

Career development
Here there was as much emphasis on maintaining career stability as

on career development, and the highest source of stress was 'worrying because of the lack of gigs'. This was the fourth highest stressor overall, and was rated a source of high pressure by 38.6 per cent of respondents. Closely related to this were 'feeling that you need to become better known and/or better paid' (28.9 per cent), and 'waiting for payment to come through from a gig or session' (27.2 per cent). 'Worrying about the lack of pensions and benefits in the music profession' was also felt to be highly stressful by 22 per cent of respondents. Lack of financial security on a day-to-day basis was, therefore, a source of extreme pressure for a large number of popular musicians.

One of the main ways that a musician's career will progress, especially if he is a pop musician, is by making records which sell, and by having a good manager to push his career. This is a perennial problem faced by the popular musician, and 32.1 per cent of respondents felt that 'finding it difficult to get a good recording or management deal for your band or musical project' was a source of high pressure.

At the other end of the spectrum, attaining fame can bring its own problems, which may reach their ultimate conclusion in a total divorce from reality. 19.5 per cent of respondents felt that 'being a member of a famous band putting special pressures on you' was a high stressor. Although it may be 'tough at the top', few musicians felt that they had reached their career ceiling, and 'feeling that you have reached the top too soon' was rated as a high pressure by only 3.2 per cent of respondents.

Few musicians, only 4.4 per cent, were worried unduly about being sacked from a gig or band, possibly because there is little of a permanent nature in popular music, and it is frequently the musician's lot to move from one musical situation to another.

Relationships at work
Interestingly, the main sources of pressure in this category were once again related to what might be termed 'the smooth running of the gig'. The biggest pressure for musicians regarding work relationships was 'having to sack a musician if you are a bandleader', with 30.5 per cent of respondents rating this a high stressor. Musicians obviously find this an unpleasant task, and it is interesting to note that it is more stressful to sack someone than to be sacked oneself. As mentioned previously, only 4.4 per cent of musicians worried excessively about being sacked.

Two main sources of tension, which detract from the smooth running of a musical engagement, are caused when a musician has to drop out at the last minute, possibly because he has a more lucrative gig, and when the musicians are travelling separately to the venue. Frayed nerves are a frequent result. 27.2 per cent of respondents felt that 'getting musicians to deputize at short notice' was a source of high pressure, while 22 per cent found that 'worrying about all the musicians getting to the gig on time' was highly stressful.

With regard to actual personality clashes, 'disagreeing with your producer or engineer in the recording studio' was rated as highly stressful by 19.5 per cent of respondents, 'personality clashes with, or jealousy of other musicians' by 19.1 per cent, and 'coping with a bandleader or musical director whose musical ideas clash with yours' by 18.3 per cent. There is thus evidence that work relationships can be highly stressful for popular musicians, although perhaps not as stressful as for classical musicians, as evidenced by the studies of Schulz (1981) and James (1984).

Role in the musical organization
The highest organizational stressor was 'as an artist, coming into conflict with recording, management or agency executives who are involved in your career and who do not share your musical ideals'. 28.5 per cent of respondents found this to be highly stressful. A large number of popular musicians are, therefore, in agreement with Hrano (1984) and Wright (1983) regarding the perennial 'artist versus businessman' conflict.

If one regards a band as an organization, then the musician may frequently find himself in a situation producing role conflict, since he may be confronted by numerous extra-musical duties, such as having to drive the band's transport, set up equipment, repair faulty amplifiers, and get engagements for the band. Thus, a considerable number of respondents, 19.5 per cent, found that 'feeling that playing is only one part of being a musician' was a source of high pressure.

Effects on social and family life
As has emerged from a review of the survey results, the popular musician appears to be single-minded and dedicated to his art, and it might not be an overstatement to say that in some cases he is 'married to his music'. There are thus bound to be certain conflicts between work and family life, and a large proportion of respondents, 30.5 per cent in all, felt that 'stress put upon personal relationships, for example, marriage, due to unusual working hours and long periods away from home' was a source of high pressure.

High stressors – conclusions

From an observation of the main sources of high pressure, it appears that the popular musician's prime concern is that he will not be able to play to the best of his ability. The highest stresses relate to the variety of problems which may stop him from doing this, for instance, his instrument not working properly, inadequate rehearsals, suffering from fatigue, and so forth. Therefore, the highest stressors overall are those which impinge directly upon performance.

Positive coping strategies
The most popular positive coping strategy utilized by popular musicians was humour, with 54.4 per cent of respondents stating that they used humour often or always. This is an interesting finding, in that it is in accord with Koestler's (1969) theory that there is a connection between humour and creativity. A number of well-known musicians have had their own TV or radio comedy shows, including the jazz trumpeter Jack Sheldon, and the rock drummer Keith Moon.

Other popular positive coping strategies were 'talking to someone you know', and 'taking exercise'. It appears, therefore, that the increased popularity of health and fitness in recent years has had an influence on popular musicians. On the other hand, the least popular measures were informal relaxation techniques, such as deep breathing, meditation and yoga, and leaving the work area. It seems that the musician feels that he can ill afford to take time off work.

Type A coronary-prone behaviour
Type A coronary-prone behaviour is characterized by extremes of competitiveness, aggressiveness, striving for achievement, impatience, and feelings of being under pressure of time and under the challenge of responsibility. Its opposite, Type B behaviour, is characterized by a low sense of time urgency, no free-floating hostility, ability to relax without guilt, etc.

The distribution of Type A and B behaviour in the general population tends to be Type A_1, 10 per cent; Type A_2, 40 per cent; Type B_3, 40 per cent, and Type B_4, 10 per cent (Rosenman et al., 1964). Type A_1 signifies the most highly developed Type A behaviour, and Type B_4, the most extreme Type B behaviour. It appears that popular musicians exhibit above-average levels of Type A behaviour. 15.8 per cent of respondents fell into the Type A_1 category, while 62.2 per cent fell into the Type A_2 category. Only 22 per cent qualified as Type B_3 personalities, while no respondents appeared in the Type B_4 category.

It was concluded earlier that the popular musician appears to be a driven individual, striving towards artistic self-satisfaction and a high level of performance. In so doing, he imposes a high level of pressure upon himself. These characteristics are in line with someone exhibiting high Type A behaviour.

General health
General health was measured by the slightly modified version of the Gurin Psychosomatic Symptom List (Gurin et al., 1960). This questionnaire yields scores ranging from 24 to 120, with a mean of 72. The higher scores are indicative of poor health. The mean score of our sample of popular musicians on this questionnaire was 53.48 (standard deviation = 13.30), and therefore there was a bias towards good general health.

In their original study using the Psychosomatic Symptom List, Gurin et al. (1960) carried out a factor analysis of the questionnaire items, and found that four striking factors emerged. They labelled these (1) psychological anxiety, (2) physical health, (3) immobilization, or psychological inertia, and (4) physical anxiety. Therefore, scores for psychological anxiety, physical health, immobilization and physical anxiety were calculated from our main sample and compared to the norms given by Gurin et al.

The main sample of popular musicians showed significantly high psychological anxiety scores compared to norms. 28 per cent of the sample were found to have high psychological anxiety scores compared to 22 per cent in the Gurin et al. sample, while 44 per cent indicated a medium psychological anxiety score compared to 28 per cent in the Gurin et al. sample. Therefore, it would appear that popular musicians as a whole suffer from above-average levels of psychological anxiety. This result coincides with the findings of the preliminary survey, in that popular musicians gained above-average scores on the neuroticism dimension of the Eysenck Personality Questionnaire, and is also in line with the study by Kemp (1981), where classical musicians were found to have above-average levels of anxiety as measured by the 16 Personality Factor Questionnaire.

On the other three factors, namely physical health, immobilization and physical anxiety, popular musicians fell within normal limits, although only 66 per cent enjoyed good physical health, as measured by low scores on this factor, compared to 81 per cent in the Gurin et al. sample. Thus, it could be stated that popular musicians enjoy generally quite good physical health, with few manifestations of physical anxiety. However, they do perceive themselves to be somewhat more psychologically anxious or worried.

Negative coping strategies
With regard to the use of drugs as an aid to relaxation, aspirins, tranquillizers or other medication did not appear to be popular among musicians, with only 2.9 per cent stating that they used aspirin 'often or always', and only 4.2 per cent stating that they used tranquillizers 'often or always'. Coffee was used frequently by 30.5

per cent and cigarettes by 30.7 per cent, but the most frequently used relaxation method was having an alcoholic drink, with 45.5 per cent of respondents stating that they imbibed on a frequent basis. Cannabis was used as a regular relaxation method by only 10.7 per cent of respondents.

Alcohol consumption It was interesting to note that, contrary to popular opinion, popular musicians did not appear to be excessively heavy drinkers (see Table 6.2). Only 14.5 per cent of respondents stated that they had more than six drinks per day (where one drink is a single whisky, gin or brandy; a glass of wine, sherry or port; or half a pint of beer). According to *Social Trends* (1986), 21 per cent of the population have six drinks or the equivalent per day.

Table 6.2 *Alcohol consumption*

	% (no.)
Teetotal	4.6 (11)
An occasional drink	24.1 (58)
Several drinks a week, but not every day	28.6 (69)
Regularly, 1 or 2 drinks a day	12.4 (30)
Regularly, 3–6 drinks a day	15.8 (38)
Regularly, more than 6 drinks a day	14.5 (35)

Cigarette smoking 39.3 per cent of respondents stated that they were currently smoking cigarettes. This appears to be slightly higher than the national average, since, according to *Social Trends* (1986) 36 per cent of the population smoke. Of those respondents who were smoking, the largest percentage (11.9 per cent) smoked 15–20 cigarettes per day.

Table 6.3 *Cigarette smoking*

	% (no.)
Never smoked	35.7 (87)
Given up smoking	25.0 (61)
Currently smoking	39.3 (96)

Use of illegal drugs It goes without saying that the use of illegal drugs is an emotionally loaded subject, and the observation may be made that the answers given in this section should be viewed with caution. However, the authors emphasized in the survey question-

Table 6.4   *Use of illegal drugs*

	Never % (no.)		Rarely % (no.)		Sometimes % (no.)		Often % (no.)		A lot % (no.)	
Cannabis	49.2	(119)	20.7	(50)	16.9	(41)	8.7	(21)	4.5	(11)
LSD	94.7	(215)	5.3	(12)						
Amphetamines	84.3	(194)	11.7	(27)	3.5	(8)			0.5	(1)
Cocaine	73.3	(173)	15.3	(36)	10.2	(24)	1.2	(3)		
Heroin	97.8	(223)	2.2	(5)						

naire that the answers would remain anonymous and strictly confidential, and were for statistical purposes. We were, therefore, prepared to accept them at face value. Given this caveat, it cannot be said from the main survey results that popular musicians overall indulge excessively in illegal drugs.

With regard to cannabis, 49.2 per cent of respondents stated that they never used it, while 20.7 per cent used it only rarely. 16.9 per cent used it sometimes, but only 13.2 per cent used it often or a lot. LSD was used only rarely, by 5.3 per cent of respondents, and amphetamines were used frequently by only 0.5 per cent. Turning to cocaine, this drug was used rarely by 15.3 per cent of respondents, sometimes by 10.2 per cent, and often by only 1.2 per cent. Heroin was only used rarely, and then by only 2.2 per cent of respondents. It thus appears that the drugs most frequently used by popular musicians are cannabis and cocaine, though not by large numbers of musicians.

Although statistics regarding drug-taking among members of the general public are lacking, a recent survey of 400 young people in the magazine *Hit* (1985) found that 52.4 per cent had used cannabis, 36.5 per cent had used amphetamines, 26 per cent had used LSD, 15 per cent had used cocaine, and 9.8 per cent had used heroin. According to *Social Trends* (1986), the highest risk of drug addiction is among young people aged twenty to twenty-four years old. There were 5,415 notifications of new addicts in the UK in 1984, and this was 30 per cent more than in 1983 and double the number in 1982. 90 per cent of new addicts notified in 1984 claimed addiction to heroin.

Therefore, compared to young people in the general population, it does not appear that popular musicians as a whole represent a high-risk group with regard to the use of illegal drugs.

Job satisfaction
The majority of respondents, 86.8 per cent, were in agreement that they found real enjoyment in their work as musicians. This result

coincides with studies of classical musicians, with James (1984) and Schulz (1981) finding that 91 per cent and 84 per cent respectively, found enjoyment in their work.

However, with regard to present gigs, respondents were less happy. 20.9 per cent of musicians were not satisfied with their current work situation, while 17 per cent were undecided. This once again points to the fact that popular musicians are often obliged to work in situations which are less than fulfilling in order to earn a living, and this factor is obviously causing individual distress and discontent.

Summary
Compared to general population norms, popular musicians do not appear to smoke cigarettes, drink alcohol, or use illegal drugs excessively, and their general level of health is quite good. However, they suffer from above-average levels of psychological anxiety, and although the majority enjoy their work as musicians, they are frequently dissatisfied with specific gigs that they have to play.

Individual profiles of sub-categories of musicians

From an observation of the data relating to the stressors and stress outcomes, distinctive profiles of each sub-category of popular musician emerged. The Kruskal-Wallis One-Way Analysis of Variance was used to ascertain whether any significant differences existed between the sub-categories with regard to the variables (see Tables 6.5, 6.6 and 6.7).

Jazz/gig musicians
Among popular musicians, the jazz musician most closely approaches the profile of the 'sensitive, dedicated artist'. He finds significantly more enjoyment in his work as a musician than other popular musicians, and his biggest source of pressure is reaching or maintaining the standards of musicianship that he sets for himself. 60.9 per cent of jazz musicians found this to be a high stressor. He suffers significantly more than other musicians from performance anxiety and related anxieties, and has the highest level of psychological anxiety. 31 per cent of jazz musicians were found to suffer from high psychological anxiety.

He is significantly more sensitive than other musicians to the ignorance of the public about music, and appears to find stressful anything which stops him 'getting on and playing creatively'. Thus, he dislikes recording sessions, the effects of over-amplified music, and being involved in non-playing responsibilities. 'Keeping up with new technology' is of minimal importance. In order to cope with stress, he uses strategies such as yoga, meditation and deep relaxation significantly more than other musicians.

Jazz musicians attained the lowest type A_1 score, at 6.4 per cent. This could be taken as further evidence that the jazz musician is less interested in achieving material success than other popular musicians, and is more inner-orientated.

Pop/gig musicians

As might be predicted, pop/gig musicians are concerned to a greater extent than other musicians with their involvement in the pop music business, and their need for commercial success. The highest stressor for pop/gig musicians, at 49.1 per cent, was 'coming into conflict with recording, management or agency executives who are involved in your career and who do not share your musical ideals', while the second highest stressor, at 48.4 per cent, was 'finding it difficult to get a good recording or management deal for your musical project'. Attaining or maintaining musical standards was rated a lower stressor than these, being rated the fourth highest source of pressure by 45.9 per cent of pop/gig musicians.

'Career development' and 'confrontations with the music business' emerge as being significantly more stressful for the pop/gig musician, as do 'work relationships', 'personal relationships' and 'personality clashes', giving the impression that he exists in a harsh, competitive environment. Physical danger is also a problem, since the pop musician's music is the most heavily amplified, yet he is significantly less worried about this than other musicians.

The problems of fame are also greatest for the pop/gig musician. 27.4 per cent rated 'if you are a member of a famous band, feeling that this puts special pressures on you' as a high stressor, and this was greater than for other groups of musicians.

He is also significantly more prone to certain health problems which manifest themselves as feelings of immobilization or inertia, and he uses more frequently than other musicians, the drugs cannabis, amphetamines and cocaine.

Commercial/gig musicians

The commercial/gig musician emerges as the 'poor relation' of the popular music world: the odd-jobber picking up work where he can. 25 per cent of this group earned less than £4,000 per annum. Worrying about the 'lack of gigs' and the 'expensiveness of instruments' are significantly more stressful for the commercial gigger than for other groups of musicians, and his highest pressure is from 'instruments not working properly', with 65 per cent of his

Table 6.5 *Sub-categories of musicians: alcohol consumption*

	Jazz/gig % (no.)		Pop/gig % (no.)		Commercial/ gig % (no.)		Pop/session % (no.)		Commercial/ session % (no.)		Commercial/ residency % (no.)	
Teetotal	4.7	(3)	3.5	(2)	10.0	(2)	2.3	(1)	7.9	(3)	16.7	(3)
An occasional drink	26.6	(17)	17.5	(10)	20.0	(4)	36.4	(16)	21.1	(8)	33.3	(6)
Several drinks a week, but not every day	32.8	(21)	28.1	(16)	45.0	(9)	15.9	(7)	26.3	(10)		
Regularly, 1 or 2 drinks a day	9.4	(6)	17.5	(10)			18.2	(8)	13.2	(5)	5.6	(1)
Regularly, 3–6 drinks a day	9.4	(6)	21.1	(12)	15.0	(3)	15.9	(7)	13.2	(5)	27.8	(5)
Regularly, more than 6 drinks a day	17.2	(11)	12.3	(7)	10.0	(2)	11.4	(5)	18.4	(7)	16.7	(3)

Table 6.6 *Sub-categories of musicians: cigarette smoking*

	Jazz/gig % (no.)		Pop/gig % (no.)		Commercial/ gig % (no.)		Pop/session % (no.)		Commercial/ session % (no.)		Commercial/ residency % (no.)	
Never smoked	26.6	(17)	33.3	(20)	40.0	(8)	45.5	(20)	39.5	(15)	38.9	(7)
Given up smoking	34.4	(22)	21.7	(13)	25.0	(5)	18.2	(8)	31.6	(12)	5.6	(1)
Currently smoking	39.0	(25)	45.0	(27)	35.0	(7)	36.4	(16)	28.9	(11)	55.6	(10)

Table 6.7 *Sub-categories of musicians: use of illegal drugs*

		Jazz/gig % (no.)	Pop/gig % (no.)	Commercial/ gig % (no.)	Pop/session % (no.)	Commercial/ session % (no.)	Commercial/ residency % (no.)
Cannabis	Never	52.4 (33)	32.2 (19)	65.0 (13)	36.4 (16)	73.7 (28)	55.6 (10)[2]
	Rarely	17.5 (11)	25.4 (15)	15.0 (3)	31.8 (14)	10.5 (4)	16.7 (3)
	Sometimes	15.9 (10)	22.0 (13)	5.0 (1)	20.5 (9)	10.5 (4)	22.2 (4)
	Often	7.9 (5)	13.6 (8)		9.1 (4)	2.6 (1)	
	A lot	6.3 (4)	6.8 (4)	15.0 (3)	2.3 (1)	2.6 (1)	5.6 (1)
LSD	Never	95.1 (58)	90.6 (48)	100.0 (18)	92.7 (38)	100.0 (37)	94.1 (16)
	Rarely	4.9 (3)	9.4 (5)		7.3 (3)		5.9 (1)
Amphetamines	Never	90.2 (55)	74.1 (40)	84.2 (16)	76.2 (32)	94.6 (35)	94.1 (16)[1]
	Rarely	6.6 (4)	20.4 (11)	15.8 (3)	19.0 (8)	2.7 (1)	5.9 (1)
	Sometimes	3.3 (2)	3.7 (2)		4.8 (2)	2.7 (1)	
	A lot		1.9 (1)				
Cocaine	Never	77.4 (48)	55.2 (32)	94.7 (18)	55.8 (24)	94.6 (35)	94.1 (16)[2]
	Rarely	14.5 (9)	22.4 (13)	5.3 (1)	27.9 (12)	2.7 (1)	
	Sometimes	8.1 (5)	19.0 (11)		14.0 (6)	2.7 (1)	5.9 (1)
	Often		3.4 (2)		2.3 (1)		
Heroin	Never	96.7 (59)	98.1 (52)	100.0 (19)	97.6 (40)	100.0 (37)	94.1 (16)
	Rarely	3.3 (2)	1.9 (1)		2.4 (1)		5.9 (1)

[1] $p < 0.05$
[2] $p < 0.001$

group rating this as a high stressor. Undoubtedly he cannot afford to buy new instruments, and has to make do with faulty ones. An indication of his insecurity is given in that he finds it significantly more stressful than other musicians to 'read and play a difficult part' at a recording session or gig.

It appears that, overall, commercial/gig musicians are the most highly stressed group. Eighteen stressors were rated 'high' by a greater percentage than other groups of musicians.

Commercial/gig musicians gained the highest percentage, 5 per cent, of poor overall health scores, between scores 97 and 120, on the Gurin Psychosomatic Symptom List, and were the highest percentage, 5.3 per cent, to say that they strongly disagreed that they found real enjoyment in their work as musicians.

Pop/session musicians

The pop/session musician stands on the middle ground between the pop/gig musician and the commercial/session musician, sharing some of the characteristics of both his fellows. He belongs to the second highest-paid group of musicians, with 30.2 per cent earning over £20,000 per annum, and is relatively unstressed. With regard to the analyses of variance showing significant differences between sub-categories of musicians relating to various stressors, pop/session musicians were ranked second lowest on eight variables, and lowest on five variables. For the pop/session musician, the highest stressor is reaching or maintaining the musical standards that he sets for himself, with 47.7 per cent finding this is a high stressor, and he has the second highest Type A_1 personality, with 23.3 per cent of his group attaining a Type A_1 score. This makes sense, since the recording session world is highly competitive. Like pop/gig musicians, pop/session musicians use cannabis, amphetamines and cocaine more than other groups of musicians.

Commercial/session musicians

Overall, the commercial/session musician presents as the most secure and least stressed of all the sub-categories of musicians. He is the highest paid, with 45.9 per cent of his group earning over £20,000 per annum, he is older, is more frequently married, and has more children. He may be best described as a well-paid craftsman, and the fact that 'the effects of noise when the music is heavily amplified' is for him the highest stressor, may reflect to some extent his conservative nature (52.7 per cent of commercial/session musicians found this to be a high pressure).

Regarding the analyses of variance showing significant differences between sub-categories of musicians relating to various stressors, the commercial/session musician was ranked lowest on eleven variables. He is the least frequent cigarette smoker, with only 28.9 per cent of his group currently smoking, and the least frequent user of illegal drugs. On the other hand, he has the highest Type A_1 personality, with 23.6 per cent of his group attaining a Type A_1 score; he is the most frequent user of tranquillizers, with 10.8 per cent taking tranquillizers 'often or always', and he is the heaviest drinker of alcohol, with 18.4 per cent of his group consuming more than six drinks per day. This again may reflect the competitive nature of the recording session world, and it is interesting to note that session musicians as a whole have the highest Type A personalities.

Commercial/residency musicians

The commercial/residency musician could be considered to be one rung up the ladder from commercial/gig musicians, since long-term residencies represent a certain stability of employment. Nevertheless, he still tends to be dissatisfied with his situation as, overall, he finds real enjoyment in his work significantly less than other groups of musicians. He is also the heaviest cigarette smoker, with 55.6 per cent of his group currently smoking, and this may reflect the boredom of his environment. The highest stressor for the commercial/residency musician is 'reaching or maintaining the musical standards' that he sets for himself, with 55.5 per cent finding this a high pressure. 'Keeping up with new technology', 'having to sack a musician' if he is a bandleader, and 'getting musicians to deputize at short notice' are all significantly more stressful for him than for other groups of musicians, and these could all be seen as workaday stressors in keeping with the nature of his musical situation.

Comparisons between individual instrumentalists

It was felt that, as well as drawing comparisons between subcategories of musicians, it would be interesting to note if any differences occurred between instrumentalists. In this respect, the main fact that emerged was that guitarists and trumpeters presented distinctive profiles. Guitarists were least concerned by the effects of 'volume' when the music is heavily amplified, and they ranked second only to pianists in terms of feeling that they have to cope with an 'instrument that is physically difficult to play'. They also felt the most stress with regard to 'personal relationships', and suffered the highest degree of psychological anxiety.

On the other hand, trumpeters had the fewest problems in playing their instrument, were ranked second lowest on pressure from personal relationships, and had the lowest degree of psychological anxiety. They also used more frequently such positive coping strategies as meditation and relaxation techniques. This profile is in broad agreement with that of other studies, such as that of Davies (1978) and Kemp (1980).

Although no significant differences were found between instrumentalists with regard to Type A personality, it was nevertheless felt that it would be interesting to make comparisons in terms of Type A_1 characteristics. Guitarists once again emerged as being highest in this respect, with 29.2 per cent exhibiting Type A_1 personalities. Trumpeters emerged as being sixth in the list of instrumentalists on this variable. The data is presented in Table 6.8.

Table 6.8 *Type A_1 personality: comparison of individual instrumentalists*

	% (no.)	
Guitarists	29.2	(10)
Pianists	25.8	(6)
Keyboardists	20.1	(3)
Vocalists	15.4	(2)
Drummers	15.4	(7)
Trumpeters	12.5	(2)
Bassists	8.1	(3)
Saxophonists	7.4	(2)
Trombonists	0.0	(0)

Female popular musicians

As has been mentioned previously, there has been a recent emphasis in occupational stress research on the special problems encountered by women in the working environment (for example, Cooper and Davidson, 1982). Therefore, thirty questionnaires were sent to female popular musicians, and fourteen questionnaires were returned. This is admittedly a small figure, but is a reflection of the fact that women are in a minority in popular music. In order to compare the statistical differences between the female and male popular musician samples in terms of their responses, two-tailed *t*-tests with the critical 5 per cent *t*-value significance level were used (Maxwell, 1970).

50 per cent of female popular musicians worked in pop music. 63 per cent of respondents were vocalists, emphasizing that this is the main role that women take in popular music. The majority of instrumentalists (21 per cent) fell into the category of jazz/gig musicians.

Female popular musicians were significantly younger than males

($p < 0.001$), and the majority (57 per cent) were unmarried. It was interesting to note that females earned significantly less than males, with 62 per cent of females earning less than £4,000 annually. They felt significantly more stressed on two stressor variables; these were 'having to read and play a difficult part at a recording session or gig' ($p < 0.05$) and 'feeling tense or nervous when doing a live gig with your regular band' ($p < 0.04$). There is thus the impression that females tend to feel less confident in 'playing situations' than their male colleagues. The highest stressor overall for female musicians, as with males, was 'feeling that you must reach or maintain the musical standards you set for yourself'. This was rated a high stressor by 57 per cent of female musicians.

With regard to stress outcomes, the only significant difference between female and male popular musicians was in relation to alcohol consumption, with males drinking significantly more ($p < 0.005$). This tends to be in line with national norms (*Social Trends*, 1986). Although, owing to the small survey sample, sweeping conclusions cannot be drawn about female musicians, the impression is that they tend to be 'second-class citizens' in the world of popular music. Although 14 per cent earned over £20,000 annually, they were overall significantly less well paid than males, and also had less confidence in their ability in playing situations.

Comments written by female musicians in the final section of the survey questionnaire were also illuminating. The following comment relates to male sexist attitudes:

> Choosing to work with a band of likeminded women musicians eases the amount of sexism I have to deal with, but it's still there, coming from publicans, agents, men in audiences, some male musicians (however hip they like to think they are), club owners, bookers, etc., etc.

Another comment reflects the home versus career dilemma:

> I find most of my friends and relations have very little understanding of my music, and tend to regard it as a wicked subterfuge to escape from my duties as a wife and mother. I feel guilty towards my husband for living largely on his income.

A further comment by a female musician is relevant to the fact that female musicians in the survey were found to be significantly younger than males:

> Age and appearance are an understated source of stress even in areas of music where they were previously less important. Females have always been subject to scrutiny in this respect, and this is an example of selection on non-musical grounds.

Therefore, as in other areas of employment, there is evidence to suggest that women may be discriminated against because of their sex.

Predictors of health risks for popular musicians

The results presented up to this point have described the high stressors and the stress outcomes for the main sample of popular musicians, and the major differences between the sub-categories of musicians. The final major analysis of the data represents an attempt to identify any stress factors which predict high levels of mental ill health, alcoholism, cigarette and drug consumption, and job dissatisfaction in popular musicians. To this end, the statistical technique of stepwise multiple regression analysis was used. However, before the analysis could be carried out, it was necessary to reduce the large number of stress variables using factor analysis. The factor analysis was carried out on the 53 items in the work stressor questionnaire, and eleven factors were extracted for interpretation. These factors, and the items which loaded significantly, are shown in Table 6.9. The other variables included in the multiple regression analysis as possible predictors were 'personal' and 'job demographics', 'positive coping strategies', and 'Type A coronary-prone behaviour'.

Table 6.9   *Factor analysis of work stressor items*

Factor 1   Performance Anxiety

Feeling tense or nervous when playing in the recording studio with your regular band
Feeling tense or nervous when playing in the recording studio as a session musician
Feeling tense or nervous when playing a live gig as a session musician
Working in the enclosed and isolated environment of the recording studio
Feeling tense or nervous when playing a live gig with your regular band
Doing an audition
Having to read and play a difficult part at a recording session or gig

Factor 2   Work over/underload related to travelling

Doing a long tour
Feeling lonely or bored in strange towns or hotels when on tour
Waiting around for long periods at the gig before it's time to play
Doing recording sessions or rehearsals during the day, then having to do a gig at night
Having to play after travelling a long distance

Factor 3   Performance-related anxiety

Worrying that your style of playing is no longer fashionable
Worrying that your ability to play will leave you
Feeling that you must reach or maintain the standards of musicianship that you set for yourself

Table 6.9   *continued*
Factor analysis of work stressor items

Feeling that your musical ability is not appreciated because of the public's ignorance about music

Feeling that you have reached the top too soon

Factor 4   Instruments and equipment

Expensiveness of instruments and other musical equipment
Coping with an instrument that is physically difficult to play
Keeping up with new equipment and technology
Instruments or equipment not working properly

Factor 5   Career development

Worrying because of the lack of gigs
Feeling that you need to become better known and/or better paid
Having to mingle socially with other musicians so that you will keep getting gigs
Finding it difficult to get a good recording or management deal for your band or musical project

Factor 6   Poor physical work conditions

Working at night, often into the early hours
Endangering your life by having to drive a long distance after a gig when you are tired
Playing at a venue with bad conditions

Factor 7   Effects on social and family life

Feeling alienated from people who lead a 'normal, everyday' lifestyle and may regard you as a 'second class citizen'
Stress put upon personal relationships
Feeling that if you are too intense or honest about your music, other musicians will regard you with suspicion

Factor 8   Playing disliked gigs

Having to do a routine, repetitive gig such as working in a theatre pit orchestra
Having to play music you don't like, in order to earn a living
Effects of noise when the music is heavily amplified
Endangering your life by having to drive a long distance after a gig when you are tired

Factor 9   Things going wrong on a gig

Worrying about all the musicians getting to the gig on time
Getting musicians to deputize at short notice
Instruments or equipment not working properly

Factor 10   Conflicts within a band

Personality clashes with, or jealousy of other musicians

Table 6.9   *continued*
Factor analysis of work stressor items

Feeling that decisions about your band's musical policy are taken without consulting
      you
If you are a member of a famous band, feeling that this puts special pressures on you

Factor 11   General relationships in the working situation

In the recording studio, disagreeing with your producer or engineer
Coping with a bandleader or musical director whose musical ideas clash with yours
Feeling that decisions about your band's musical policy are taken without consulting
      you
Having to sack a musician if you are a bandleader

General health

Six variables significantly predicted ill health for the main sample of popular musicians. These were Factor 3 (performance-related anxiety), Factor 6 (poor physical work conditions), Factor 1 (performance anxiety), Factor 2 (work over/underload related to travelling), Factor 7 (effects on social and family life), and 'not taking exercise'. Therefore, the main predictors of ill health for popular musicians as a whole are those which affect musical performance. It appears significant that performance-related anxiety plays such a large part: there is the suggestion that there exist in the mind of the musician ever-present doubts and misgivings, leading to a state of above average psychological anxiety, which in turn can undermine his physical health. This is in line with the hypothesis put forward by Carruthers (1969), which proposed that emotion, through enhanced activity of the sympathetic nervous system, can result in physical processes which may lead to such illnesses as coronary heart disease.

Cigarette smoking

Four variables significantly predicted cigarette smoking, and three of these concerned the non-use of positive coping strategies, namely 'not taking exercise', 'not talking to someone you know', and 'not taking time out'. In effect, a negative strategy is chosen instead of positive ones. The fourth predictor of increased cigarette smoking was low salary. It may be the case, therefore, that feelings of frustration caused by low income, are expressed to some extent by an increase in smoking.

Alcohol consumption

Only one variable, Factor 3 (performance-related anxiety), significantly predicted high alcohol consumption, although the amount of variance predicted was extremely small. Hence, this variable cannot be classified as a statistically strong predictor of drinking in popular musicians. It can only be assumed that alcohol consumption takes place largely for social reasons, rather than for purposes of stress reduction, and it is also necessary to take into account the fact that, as stated earlier, popular musicians do not appear to be excessively heavy drinkers compared to the general public.

Use of illegal drugs

For four of the drugs, namely LSD, amphetamines, cocaine and heroin, no significant predictors of usage were obtained, and it is likely that this is due to the fact that the majority of popular musicians used these drugs rarely, if at all. However, four variables significantly predicted cannabis use. These were Factor 11 (general relationships in the work situation), 'turning professional at an early age', 'having few children', and 'having few educational qualifications'.

In conceptualizing these predictors of cannabis use, it appears that a musician who is likely to use cannabis frequently is one who has come into conflict with his work colleagues, and who wishes to block out the stressful effects of this experience. He is likely to have become a professional musician at an early age, and, due to youthful inexperience, may have succumbed to the influence of his peer group in using cannabis. He has few, if any children, and is therefore likely to be at the younger end of the age range, and also has few, if any, educational qualifications. One may speculate, therefore, that the cannabis-smoking popular musician is young, may have difficulty articulating his feelings due to a lack of education, and when he experiences problems in asserting himself in an argument with colleagues, he withdraws via drug use. There is some support for this hypothesis in that, according to *Social Trends* (1986), the highest drug usage occurs among young people aged twenty to twenty-four.

Lack of job satisfaction

Four factors significantly predicted job dissatisfaction. These were Factor 5 (lack of career development), Factor 9 (things going wrong on a gig), Type B behaviour, and Factor 3 (performance-related anxiety). It was extremely interesting to find that the third predictor of job dissatisfaction in the main sample of popular musicians was a low Type A behaviour score or, in other words, the exhibiting of non-assertive, less competitive and less time-directed behaviour. This appears to contradict the findings of much of the literature on occupational stress, which shows that high Type A behaviour can lead to detrimental outcomes such as coronary heart disease (for example, Rosenman et al., 1964). However, it was stated earlier that popular musicians as a whole exhibit above-average Type A behaviour, and this may be intrinsic to their nature. It is possible that positive aspects of Type A behaviour, such as drive, ambition for personal satisfaction, and the desire to attain self-imposed musical standards, contribute to job satisfaction, and a musician low on these characteristics might therefore experience a sense of unfulfilment, expressed as job dissatisfaction.

In conclusion, the popular musician who lacks job satisfaction appears to be one who is concerned about financial stability and career development, who finds that his gigs do not run smoothly due to various setbacks and to performance-related anxiety, and who lacks personal drive.

Stress vulnerability profiles

A series of multiple regression analyses was also carried out with the sub-categories of popular musicians in an attempt to ascertain the predictors of ill health. Since the number of musicians in each sub-category was relatively small, certain of the sub-categories were amalgamated to form sub-groups containing larger numbers for the multiple regression analyses. Thus, while the sub-category 'jazz/gig musicians' remained as previously, the sub-categories 'pop/gig musicians' and 'pop/session musicians' were combined to form a new sub-category entitled 'pop musicians', while the sub-categories 'commercial/gig musicians', 'commercial/session musicians' and 'commercial/residency musicians' were combined to form a new sub-category entitled 'commercial musicians'.

In the present section, the distinctive independent and dependent variables and predictors of ill health are presented graphically for each group of popular musicians, and the main factors implicated in the prediction of mental ill health are discussed.

Main sample of popular musicians
From an observation of the data relating to popular musicians as a whole (Figure 6.1), the individual most at risk in relation to psychosomatic ill health is someone who experiences high levels of performance and performance-related anxiety. He frequently has to play in poor physical work conditions, and regularly endures the boredom, loneliness and fatigue associated with touring and travelling. He is also suffering from high pressure in his social and

Stressors

Keeping up musical standards (highest stressor)
Instruments not working
Read and play difficult part
Lack of gigs
Inadequate rehearsals
Effects of loud music
Driving when tired
Trying for a good deal
Sacking a musician
Pressure on relationships

High Type A behaviour

↓

Stress outcomes

High psychological anxiety
Dissatisfaction with present gigs

↓

Predictors of mental ill health

Performance-related anxiety
Poor physical work conditions
Performance anxiety
Work over/underload related to travelling
Effects on social and family life
Not taking exercise

Figure 6.1   *Popular musicians as a whole: their stressors, stress outcomes and factors that predict mental ill health*

family life, and does not use physical exercise as a means of maintaining health.

Jazz musicians
Stress factors for jazz musicians are shown in Figure 6.2. The jazz musician is obviously aware that he is taking a risk in playing music which gives him a high level of enjoyment, since he tends to turn pro later in life, covers himself by teaching music more frequently and by having another job more frequently, and is the most acutely aware of the public's ignorance about music.

The jazz musician most likely to suffer from psychosomatic ill health symptoms is one who does not use humour or take exercise, who suffers from frequent problems with his instruments and equipment, and who experiences high levels of performance anxiety.

Stressors

Best higher educational qualifications
Turn professional later
Teach music more frequently
More frequent other job
Keeping up musical standards (highest stressor)
Tense and nervous in recording sessions
Ignorance of public
Effects of loud music
Non-playing responsibilities
Lowest interest in new technology

Lowest Type A Scores
Most frequent users of yoga, meditation and relaxation

$\downarrow$

Stress outcomes

Highest psychological anxiety
Highest work enjoyment

$\downarrow$

Predictors of ill health

Not using humour
Not taking exercise
Problems with instruments and equipment
Performance anxiety

Figure 6.2   *Jazz musicians: their stressors, stress outcomes and predictors of mental ill health*

Pop musicians
The pop/gig musician, whose stress factors are shown in Figure 6.3, is distinctive in that he is most frequently exposed to an atmosphere of hostile competitiveness, which is largely due to his involvement in the rock/pop music business. He clashes with businessmen, fellow musicians, music journalists, and in his personal relationships, and his health is at risk from a distinctive profile of stress outcomes. Rather than expressing his feelings regarding various personality clashes, he tends not to confide in those close to him and instead withdraws or gives himself confidence with the use of illegal drugs. Regarding scores on the Psychosomatic Symptom List, he has difficulty getting out of bed and getting going, and is thus more prone than other popular musicians to feelings of immobilization or depression.

In comparison, the pop/session musician is relatively unstressed.

Pop/gig musicians

Stressors
Youngest
Least frequently married
Clash with businessmen (highest stressor)
Trying for a good deal
Need to be better paid
Being in a famous band
Personality clashes
Criticism in music press
Not consulted re music
Pressure on relationships
Least worried re effects of loud music
Smoke cannabis to relax

↓

Stress outcomes
Don't feel like eating
Difficulty getting up
Smoke, drink or eat too much
Can't get going
Use cannabis, amphetamines and cocaine

Pop/session musicians

Stressors
Second highest income

Keeping up musical standards (highest stressor)
Lowest stressed on five variables

Second highest Type A scores

↓

Stress outcomes

Use cannabis, amphetamines and cocaine

↘   ↙

Predictors of mental ill health
Performance-related anxiety
Performance anxiety
Not confiding in a friend
Conflicts within a band

Figure 6.3 · *Pop musicians: their stressors, stress outcomes and predictors of mental ill health*

He is the second highest paid of popular musicians, is ranked second lowest on eight stressor variables, and lowest on five variables.

Overall, the pop musician most likely to succumb to psycho-somatic ill-health symptoms is one who experiences high levels of performance and performance-related anxiety, frequent conflicts with his band, and who does not confide in friends.

Commercial musicians
Like the pop/gig musician, the commercial/gig musician is in his own way distinctive, and, for him, three factors stand out: lowest income, poorest overall psychosomatic health, and low work enjoyment (see Figure 6.4). He is struggling to make a living, and because he must accept any gig which comes his way, work

Commercial/gig musicians	Commercial/residency musicians	Commercial/session musicians
Stressors	*Stressors*	*Stressors*
Lowest income		Highest income
		Oldest
		Most frequently married
		Has most children
Instruments not working (highest stressor)	Keeping up musical standards (highest stressor)	Effects of loud music (highest stressor)
Expensiveness of instruments	New technology	Lowest stressed on eleven variables
Lack of gigs	Sacking a musician	
Read and play difficult part	Getting deps. at short notice	Highest Type A scores
↓	↓	↓
Stress outcomes	*Stress outcomes*	*Stress outcomes*
Poorest overall Gurin health score	Heaviest cigarette smoker	Least frequent cigarette smoker
Low enjoyment in work	Lowest work enjoyment	Least frequent user of illegal drugs
		Most frequent user of tranquillizers
		Heaviest consumption of alcohol

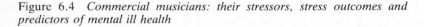

Predictors of mental ill health
Effects on social and family life
Instruments and equipment
Poor physical work conditions
Annual salary

Figure 6.4 *Commercial musicians: their stressors, stress outcomes and predictors of mental ill health*

enjoyment may be minimal. He has problems with the tools of his trade – his instruments – because he cannot afford to buy new, better ones, and his overall health is affected by the strain of 'just getting by'.

The commercial/residency musician is in a somewhat more secure position than the commercial/gig musician, and the stresses of simply making a living are replaced by the humdrum, workaday stresses of the residency situation. For the commercial/residency musician, security can tend to equal boredom. He has the heaviest cigarette consumption and lowest work enjoyment of all popular musicians.

The commercial/session musician may be described as a crafts-man who is secure, well paid, middle-aged, family orientated and conservative. Although he is the least stressed of all the sub-groups of popular musicians, this is not to say that he is unstressed, since he is the most frequent user of tranquillizers and the heaviest consumer of alcohol. It is interesting to note that the 'drug of choice' varies with age, since he is the least frequent user of illegal drugs, while the pop/gig musician is the most frequent user.

Overall, the commercial musician most likely to suffer from poor mental and physical health is one who experiences high levels of stress in his social and family life, has frequent problems with his instruments and equipment, frequently works in poor conditions, and is poorly paid.

The relevance of personality factors to the effects of stress on popular musicians

In attempting to gain as full a picture as possible with regard to vulnerability to stress, it is necessary to take into account personality factors.

In the preliminary survey, it was found that, with regard to scores on the Eysenck Personality Questionnaire, popular musicians gained above-average scores on the dimensions of neuroticism and psychoticism. It was decided that popular musicians resembled classical musicians with regard to neuroticism, as supported by the studies of Kemp (1980, 1981), where above-average levels of anxiety were found both in student and professional classical musicians. It may be that above-average neuroticism or anxiety is intrinsic to the musician's personality, since it manifests itself at an early age, at school or college.

With regard to elevated psychoticism scores, popular musicians also appear to resemble creative personalities in other fields. The study by Gotz and Gotz (1979a,b) found that professional artists had above-average psychoticism and neuroticism scores.

Results from our study of popular musicians tended to confirm those of the preliminary survey, since musicians obtained above-average scores on the psychological anxiety factor of the Gurin Psychosomatic Symptom List. There is thus evidence that popular musicians resemble classical musicians and members of other creative professions. It was also found that the 'use of humour' was the main coping strategy used by popular musicians, and this could be taken as further evidence of them fitting into the category of the creative personality, when one takes into account the link between humour and creativity discussed by Koestler (1969).

Further pointers to the personality of the popular musician are given when observing the data relating to high stressors. 'Factors intrinsic to the job' produced the highest source of pressure overall, and it was felt that the highest stressors were those which impinged directly on performance. A picture emerged of a single-minded individual, driven towards the goal of artistic self-satisfaction. This was supported by the fact that the number one stressor was 'feeling that you must reach or maintain the standards of musicianship that you set for yourself'. Also tying in with this, popular musicians gained above-average Type A behaviour scores. It has been found that high Type A's set ambiguous and high standards for themselves (Matthews, 1982), and drive themselves hard towards self-imposed goals (Burman et al., 1975; Glass, 1977; Matthews, 1982).

This may go some way to explaining why, in our multivariate analysis, high Type A behaviour scores predicted high job satisfaction. The main satisfaction was probably obtained in reaching self-imposed musical goals. A further question which arises is that relating to why, in the main study, high Type A behaviour did not predict poor health outcomes. Type A behaviour has been found to cluster into groups of different behaviours, and the main behaviours associated with illnesses such as coronary heart disease are felt to be those relating to hostile competitiveness, impatience, irritation, and vigorous voice stylistics (Dembroski and MacDougall, 1982). In popular musicians, Type A behaviour appears to be manifested mainly in terms of striving for self-imposed goals, rather than in hostile competitiveness. The musician is competing with himself as much as with his fellows. The main exception to this appears to be with pop/gig musicians, where conflicts with colleagues do appear to be implicated in specific poor health outcomes.

Thus, one is drawn to the conclusion that, for the popular musician, to a not inconsiderable extent, both pressure and pleasure arise from the characteristics of his own personality. In many ways he creates his own stress, but this is all part and parcel of being a creative artist.

7
Being at the top: the unique problems of successful rock musicians

The life of a successful rock musician can bring with it extreme and specific problems. Although several of these pressures have been discussed in previous chapters, it is helpful to turn to the popular literature on this subject in order to present as full a picture as possible.

The success of British groups in the 1960s, spearheaded by the Beatles, brought about the phenomenon of unprecedentedly intensive international touring schedules, with the frequently accompanying phenomenon of mass hysteria. Norman (1981), in his biography of the Beatles, describes their tour schedule in 1964, which included Scandinavia, Holland, the Far East, Australasia and America. The American tour, which played only large venues such as sports centres, covered 23 cities, and more than 600 miles were travelled per day. It was estimated that eventually over 22,000 miles had been covered. Everywhere the Beatles were assailed by hordes of fans, and Norman (1981) reports that when they arrived at San Francisco airport, they were driven straight from the plane into an iron cage to afford them protection. Seconds after they left it at their destination, it was crushed by the over-enthusiastic crowd.

Led Zeppelin were one of the most successful British bands of the 1970s, and as Welch (1984) describes, they were known to play for six nights per week uninterruptedly for periods of a month. In one fifteen-month period, six tours of the United States, all played to capacity crowds, were carried out. The obvious, and often documented (for example, Herman, 1982) result of non-stop touring is total disorientation, with nothing to do in anonymous hotel rooms, and a build-up of tension to the next gig. Ill health is a frequent result of such punishing schedules, and Welch (1984), in his biography of Led Zeppelin, discusses how guitarist Jimmy Page was frequently close to nervous and physical breakdown, and suffered from attacks of nausea and diarrhoea. At the end of Zeppelin's fifth American tour, vocalist Robert Plant collapsed with exhaustion. Drummer John Bonham, despite having an ostensibly extroverted personality, admitted that as Zeppelin became more successful, he suffered from constant nervousness, and attributed this to factors such as sometimes having to sit around for a whole day before a concert. On a similar note, Pete Townshend of The Who described how drummer Keith Moon was frequently sick with fear as he climbed the stairs from the dressing room to the stage (Barnes, 1982). Significantly, both Moon and Bonham died as a result of alcoholism. John Bonham is quoted as saying:

> I've got worse – terrible bad nerves all the time. Once we start into 'Rock and Roll' I'm fine. I just can't stand sitting around, and I worry about playing badly and if I do then I'm really pissed off. If I play well, I feel fine. Everybody in the band is the same and each has some little thing they do before we go on, like pacing about or lighting a cigarette. It's worse at festivals. (Welch, 1984)

Barnes (1982) describes a terrifying experience which befell Pete Townshend at the first of a series of concerts at Madison Square Gardens, New York. Over the years, Townshend had perfected a crowd-pleasing stage routine which, as well as playing, included leaping in the air and smashing his guitar. As he looked at the audience, he suddenly had the experience of not knowing what he was doing there, and was transfixed with stage fright. He managed to finish the show, but was only able to complete the series of concerts with the assistance of copious amounts of alcohol. Townshend is quoted as saying:

> I looked down into the front row and there were all these kids squealing, 'Jump, Pete, jump, jump, jump.' As if I was Pavlov's dog or some performing seal. And I panicked and I was lost. It was the most incredible feeling, after twenty years or whatever, more than half my life, to suddenly go blank. The other three shows I was terrified, I got smashed, or I couldn't have gone on. (Barnes, 1982)

Despite fame, or indeed because of it, successful rock musicians may be frequently subjected to hostility from various quarters. While touring in Sweden and Holland in 1970, Led Zeppelin were barred from several hotels and restaurants because of their long hair (Welch, 1984). The unprecedented speed of the band's rise to fame, from their inception in 1968, was a cause of resentment and jealousy, and they frequently received scathing reviews in the rock music press. This was partly due to the fact that, at least initially, they avoided interviews and publicity, preferring to find success on their own merits, and knowing that the music press often attempt 'to make and break' a band regardless of talent. Bill Harry, who was Zeppelin's public relations man, is quoted by Welch (1984) as saying that excellent concerts by the band were regularly given bad reviews in the music papers. Welch himself was present at a concert given by Led Zeppelin at the Knebworth Festival in 1979, which he felt to be superb. He was later dismayed to read a review in a leading Sunday newspaper describing them as the worst band in the world.

Perhaps the classic example of the involvement of the press with a rock star has been that of Boy George, former vocalist with the band Culture Club. As Brown (1987) describes, during his rise to fame George was an avid seeker of publicity, and the press were eager to oblige. But when it was discovered that George was a heroin addict, the tide turned, and the press stridently declared themselves to be the arbiters of morality.

The Rolling Stones have incurred a great deal of wrath, as Norman (1984) notes. Following a tour of America in 1969, they were widely accused of rock star arrogance, since it was felt that they kept their audiences waiting, and cheated them by charging exorbitant prices for tickets. Again, the music press was involved in proliferating this bad feeling, and, in fact, other bands were charging similar prices for tickets at the time. However, the Stones decided to make amends by giving a free concert, and in so doing, they unwittingly set in motion the circumstances for one of the most unfortunate events in rock history. The venue for the free concert was the Altamont speedway track in California, and from the beginning the event was organized badly, one of the main problems being that a group of Hell's Angels was employed to keep over-enthusiastic fans at bay. The Angels beat up members of the audience and the vocalist of a support band, and during the Stones' performance, in front of the stage they stabbed to death a black youth who had supposedly been brandishing a gun. Three other people died due to various circumstances during the course of the festival.

Unruly behaviour by audience members has been a constant factor accompanying the performances of successful rock musicians. Welch (1984) describes how police in Milan were involved in a pitched battle with 15,000 Led Zeppelin fans, and their tours of America and Germany were also frequently disrupted by violence. One of the worst incidents of this type occurred immediately prior to a concert given by The Who in Cincinnati in 1979. As Herman (1982) states, about 8,000 fans were still waiting to gain admittance to the concert hall at 7 p.m. when the show was due to start only an hour later. The fans broke into the hall, and in a rush to obtain seats close to the stage, eleven people were crushed to death and eight people were injured. The Who were later summoned to give depositions in law suits which arose from the tragedy (Barnes, 1982).

Successful rock bands have always had more than their fair share of hangers-on. This was never more clearly in evidence than in the case of the Beatles' Apple organization (Norman, 1981), where every manner of bizarre character was allowed into the head-quarters at 3 Savile Row. The various divisions of Apple, including Apple Films, Apple Press, Apple Retail, The Apple Foundation for the Arts, and Apple Electronics, were notably unproductive, and it was eventually discovered that money and equipment were system-atically being stolen from the Apple offices. The controversial music-business accountant, Allen Klein, was called in to sort out the Beatles' affairs.

Pete Townshend of The Who found himself in a similar position (Barnes, 1982). His Eel Pie group of companies, including The Magic Bus Bookshop and the Eel Pie equipment hire company, was run by incompetent staff, and Townshend found himself on the verge of bankruptcy. An accountant was called in and severe cuts were introduced, including the loss of twenty employees.

The rock star is frequently the focus of often unhealthy adulation by fans and this phenomenon is documented by Herman (1982). In the 1970s the era of the look-alike blossomed, and part of the attraction of attending rock concerts was to look as much as possible like one's idol, for instance David Bowie. Some fans even went to the lengths of undergoing plastic surgery to achieve this aim. Tragic extremes have sometimes been reached, as when the murderer Charles Manson decided that the lyrics of the Beatles' song 'Helter Skelter' gave credence to his deranged beliefs. The ultimate horror for the rock musician occurs when he becomes the victim of his own fan, as when John Lennon was shot by Mark Chapman in New York in 1980.

Even when not involved in such confrontations, the rock musician may be walking on a knife-edge of a different kind. At one moment he is successful, while in the next he may be thrown into total oblivion. Perhaps the classic example here is that of Pete Best, the original drummer with the Beatles. As Norman (1981) relates, Best had worked with the Beatles for two years as they built up their reputation both in Liverpool and in Germany. When they audi-tioned with EMI records, producer George Martin was not enamoured of Best's drumming, but Best did not find out until some months later, when he was sacked by Brian Epstein, the Beatles' manager. The Beatles in the meantime had said nothing to Best, and with a new drummer, Ringo Starr, they of course went on to become the most famous group of all time. Best eventually gave up playing, and was last heard of working for the Civil Service.

There are innumerable examples of this phenomenon. Frame (1974) recounts how Jeff Beck, acknowledged as one of the greatest of rock guitarists, used six different drummers – Viv Prince, Roger Cook, Rod Coombs, Aynsley Dunbar, Micky Waller and Tony Newman – in the band which he led between 1967 and 1969. Tobler and Grundy (1983) refer to Rainbow, the band led by guitarist Ritchie Blackmore. The band had a five-piece line-up, and apart from Blackmore himself, seventeen different musicians played in the band in the space of seven years.

During a highly successful tour in 1973, David Bowie announced at the end of a concert at Hammersmith Odeon that this was the last show that he and his band would ever do. As Gillman and Gillman (1986) state, the band were more shocked than the audience, since they had not been informed of this fact. A further trauma awaited the band's drummer, Woody Woodmansey, who had been expecting to go with Bowie to Paris to record a new album. On the day of his wedding, he was informed by Bowie's management that his services were no longer required.

It is thus apparent that the career of a successful rock musician is not for the faint-hearted, and the stresses inherent in the lifestyle are many and varied.

8
The future for popular musicians

In observing some of the remarks made by musicians in their returned questionnaires, the authors were drawn to the conclusion that in certain ways the concept of the study was too narrow: in the type of questions asked regarding stressors, the true essence of the popular musician had not been entirely captured. This relates to the comment made earlier that in many ways the musician creates his own stress, since this is intrinsic to being a creative artist – as one musician in our sample suggested:

> Interesting though your project concerning musicians' stress is, I have to say that for me you're approaching the situation from the wrong side. Of course I, like most people, have felt all the suggested stress points in your questionnaire to some degree and at some time or another. *But* this is all part of the creative artist's life. Travelling ridiculous hours for dubious rewards is what makes the life different from the assembly line at Ford's. Of course I would rather be well paid, but to be honest I have found that the more secure financially I am, the less interesting music I produce. I think if you asked musicians if they would rather have a boring well-paid job or a doubtful creative one the majority would choose the latter. As for stress clinics . . . it comes back to the old question of is it better to be a happy vegetable or a neurotic artist? Should Van Gogh have been provided with a stress clinic? No, I don't know either. I suppose you could say that, like bullfighters or racing drivers, musicians provide an interesting spectacle for the punters, at quite considerable danger to themselves physically and mentally. If they were entirely sane and normal they wouldn't do it.

Another musician remarked: 'Doctors, social workers will *never* understand creative artists. Even supposing one does – he can't help. Did psychoanalysis ever cure anybody?' Though somewhat pessimistic, this comment provides food for thought.

The musician takes a sort of existential stance: he is an active agent who chooses to be a musician because he feels the need, as a creative person. In doing so, he accepts any problems inherent in the job, because he has the overriding desire to play above all else.

The authors feel that the stressors and stress outcomes which have been pinpointed in the study are important and relevant with regard to the well-being of the popular musician. However, perhaps it is necessary to look at problems on a more global level, in other words, from the point of view of the popular musician's place in society.

With this in mind, it is worth looking at the qualitative comments made by a number of musicians during our study. In summary, the points are as follows:

1 The popular musician is treated as a social outcast.
2 He has little legal backing, and can be 'robbed' indiscriminately, for instance, by businessmen.
3 He cannot get help from his government.
4 He suffers from the problems of being self-employed: he cannot say exactly what his income will be, and therefore, bank managers etc. are loath to give him overdrafts, mortgages and loans.
5 He cannot fill in forms because he does not fit the questions.
6 Job centres do not have jobs to suit his skills.
7 He does not qualify, except at tax time.
8 The public has no idea of his lifestyle. He is only judged by the amount of money he makes.
9 The Musicians' Union is the only Union which has a large percentage of semi-professional members. No musical standards are set whereby someone qualifies to be a member.

An attempt will be made to address these points, and others raised by the study, in the following sections.

Popular musicians and the pop music business

As Frith (1983) states, 'the relationship between making music and making money remains . . . the musicians' central problem'. It is a fact that musicians and bands continue to experience severe problems with regard to their contracts with record companies, music publishers, managers, agents and promoters. Much light is thrown on this topic in a recent book by Garfield (1986), which demonstrates that pop musicians have been, and continue to be 'ripped off' in a period which goes back to the early 1960s. To name just a few recent cases: Elton John was in court over publishing contracts in 1985, Gilbert O'Sullivan was in court over his early recording and publishing deals in 1982, Joan Armatrading was in court over her management deal in 1985, and Wham were in court over their record deal in 1984.

Why do musicians continue to sign contracts that give them such poor financial returns for their work? Garfield (1986) gives a colourful, but succinct explanation:

You want to be like The Beatles. That is, you'd *kill* to be like them. Your ego demands the glory, your bank manager demands the money and your friends say you won't do it. And you haven't done it yet, after two years. After two years of cruddy gigs, fuddy demo tapes, and too many people laughing at your loopy trousers and your band's name and the hashed logo sprayed onto the bass drum. You've some topper songs and some burning guitar runs and all that great stuff, but no real job, no security, no respect, no influence and really nothing to show at all. You get offered that dream deal, and the last thing you want after those two years is to wait any longer. You don't wish to discover that the deal's not quite all it could be, because not only is that a blow to your ego, but it could lead to no deal at all. Worse, you don't want some legal man in a three piece explaining things like foreign publishing deals at source, when all you want is to start trying out those studio Fairlight marvels. And if he says, 'Don't sign this!', you maybe look for a new lawyer and sign while in transition. (Garfield, 1986)

It is worth looking in more detail at some of the cases which Garfield (1986) describes. For instance, the singer/songwriter Gilbert O'Sullivan, in signing a contract with his manager, Gordon Mills, did not even look at it. He felt that 'if you respect somebody, and they're going to manage you, then you have to trust them'. The deal which O'Sullivan signed with Mills' MAM record company could run to at least five years, and provided a royalty, even when successful, of a low 5 per cent in the UK and only 3½ per cent elsewhere. Still worse, there was no mention of any advance on royalties, and he received no independent legal advice.

Another example is that of the singer Hazel O'Connor, who, in 1978, finding herself in dire financial straits, signed a contract with Albion Records against legal advice. She received no advance on signing, and only £2,000 on the delivery of her first album. This was the only album to carry any contractual advance, and given that royalties may often take up to a year to be paid, it was quite insufficient to maintain even the most frugal standard of living. Royalty rates were set at 5 per cent of all releases in the UK and US, and at 4 per cent in the rest of the world. This, too, was an alarmingly low rate for the time. The contract contained many other unsatisfactory clauses. A protracted court case between O'Connor and Albion Records ensued in 1982, but the outcome was unsatisfactory for both parties, and O'Connor, whose career was at one time blossoming, has now faded into relative obscurity.

The prime aim of the pop music business is to make money, and, as such, it is undoubtedly tough and ruthless, although in actual fact probably no more so than many other businesses. Allen Klein, ex-business manager of the Rolling Stones and the Beatles, is quoted as saying:

Look, you have to survive, you do whatever it takes, because if you don't stay alive in this business you can't help anybody . . . there's only one thing that gives me an edge: I'm the best. I know more about this business than anybody else . . . It's really like chess, knowing all the moves. It's a game, for Chrissakes, and winning is everything. It's a shame it has to get nasty sometimes. (Garfield, 1986)

The evidence is that bands and musicians repeatedly sign contracts without knowing what they are doing, through naivety and a desire to 'make it'. There is now a growing body of lawyers, solicitors and accountants who specialize in pop music business matters, and as an example of this, an article by Diamond (1986) is devoted to the accountancy firm of Lubbock Fine Ltd, who now have 3,000 musicians on their books. If popular musicians are to find their dealings with the pop music business less stressful, it is essential that they become more aware of business aspects, and seek out experienced professional advice before signing contracts.

Popular musicians and the need for stress management

Although, from the results of the main survey, popular musicians do not appear to suffer from performance anxiety to the same extent as do classical musicians, nevertheless 'performance anxiety' and 'performance-related anxiety' were found to be two of the main predictors of ill health. As mentioned earlier, Black (1984b) states that there is no official recognition, and no responsibility taken by the pop music industry for the stresses of the musician's lifestyle. In a statement to the press regarding the arrest of pop star Boy George in 1986, Richard Branson, head of the Virgin Record Company, stated that Virgin Records had a health advisory service which had been in existence for seventeen years to help people with drug and psychiatric problems. However, in a personal communication with the authors, Branson (1986) stated that the service to which he referred was the Help Advisory Centre. This is actually a free confidential service and counselling centre for people of all ages, which began as a telephone advice line for students seeking advice on pregnancy and abortion, and then as a similar advice line for anyone. There does not therefore appear to be a health advisory service specifically attached to Virgin Records, nor to any other record company.

Patterson (1986) reports that her Neuro Electric Therapy represents a new cure for drug addiction. An electrical current is used to stimulate the body's supply of endorphins, enabling addicts to detoxify with minimal withdrawal symptoms. Patterson claims to have cured the rock stars Eric Clapton, Keith Richards and Pete

Townshend of heroin addiction. However, it appears that her cure is available only to those rich enough to afford it.

Reference was made earlier to the International Society for the Study of Tension in Performance. This is an organization dedicated to the investigation and treatment of every aspect of physical and psychological tension in the performing arts, and has among its members several distinguished musicians, music teachers, psychologists and physicians. The society holds regular conferences and publishes a learned journal. A member of the committee, Dr Richard Pearson, runs a private musicians' clinic. In a personal communication with the authors, Pearson (1986) stated that both the society and the clinic were concerned only with the problems of classical musicians. More recently the society has expressed a welcome interest in broadening its scope.

Although the popular musician does not suffer to the same extent from problems such as 'performance anxiety' and 'overuse injuries' as do classical musicians, these problems are still detrimental to his health, and there is thus a place for formal training for popular musicians in stress management techniques. It is not entirely necessary for the popular musician to be simply either a happy vegetable or a neurotic artist.

The Musicians' Union and the promotion of popular music

In the present section, the role of the Musicians' Union in helping the lot of the popular musician is discussed, and also certain problems which arise in so doing.

Frith (1983) makes some interesting points regarding the British Musicians' Union. He observes that the union tends to regard the bulk of its members as 'routine' musicians selling 'routine' services, and it therefore focuses on their interests rather than those of highly acclaimed 'star' musicians. The union resembles its fellow body the American Federation of Musicians in that it came into being as a result of the concerns of dance band and orchestra musicians of the 1920s and 1930s. Its main aim is to establish acceptable conditions in the clubs, cabarets, orchestras, theatres, and radio, television and recording sessions that provide the work environments for 'routine' musicians, and minimum rates of pay are negotiated and updated.

Frith (1983) points out that a further union assumption has been that as recording developed, it posed a threat to the employment of musicians, since they are regarded as being mainly live performers. In the union's view, recording provides an exceptional source of work for the 'routine' musician, and is not regarded as being at the heart of popular musical success. In its dealings with record producers, the union concerns itself mainly with the rights of session musicians in terms of negotiating set recording fees, rather than with the rights of artists or bands who have a contract with a record company. There has been a slowness to develop methods of protecting musicians from exploitation by record companies in the ways that they are protected from exploitation by 'live' employers such as agents and promoters. Therefore, the union's assumptions that musicians are mainly 'routine' workers performing in live situations have led, until recently, to a neglect of the needs of its rock and pop performers.

A further problem which has developed over the past number of years is that, due to the recession, theatres, ballrooms and cabaret clubs have closed down, and one of the few venues at which the 'standard' popular musician can play, either in his own group or in a resident backing group, is the working men's club. Unfortunately, working men's clubs are loath to pay musicians the standard Musicians' Union rate for their services, and so musicians are frequently faced with the dilemma of either working for less than the union rate or turning down a gig. There is a tendency for substandard musicians, who are willing to play for low fees, to work in these clubs, and consequently the standard of music is lowered. One possible solution to this problem suggested in correspondence to the *Musicians' Union Journal* (Baker, 1984) is that Musicians' Union officials should make a round of working men's clubs and find out how many musicians in resident backing groups are actually union members. They should then attempt to agree rates of pay with the clubs through the Trade Union Congress (TUC), to which the working men's clubs are affiliated.

A topic which frequently arises among musicians is that the Musicians' Union does not set any standard of musicianship in order to gain entry to the union, and it is often mentioned that a grading system of musical ability should be introduced. This is a problematic issue, in that it may militate against musicians who have great natural ability in certain musical areas, but not in others. At the present time this issue remains unresolved. In a personal communication with the authors, the American Federation of Musicians (Bonagiano, 1986) stated that they, like the British Musicians' Union, do not use a grading system.

On a more positive note, Morton (1986) discusses the ways in which the Musicians' Union is attempting to help musicians. The Musicians' Union is asked to help in the promotion of a wider range of music than probably any other funding organization in the United Kingdom. Decisions are carried out by the Music Promotion and Public Relations Committee, and in a typical year direct financial assistance will be given to approximately four hundred different music organizations, leading to the consequent creation of jobs for thousands of union members.

One of the main problems that the union has attempted to combat is the use of discos which replace live music. A 'Keep Music Live' campaign was initiated, and the development of more efficient complaints systems has led to increased employment of musicians in venues where discos were previously used. Morton (1986) makes the point that the British Musicians' Union is the only union in the world that is able to restrict to any degree the public use of gramophone records. Union action has also increased the level of employment of musicians in broadcasting, especially in the area of independent broadcasting.

A union employment promotion officer has been appointed to help the ordinary working musician, and to encourage union branches to examine ways and means of stimulating employment in the entertainment sector. One aspect of this has been the setting up of showcase events, where bands can perform in front of an invited audience of agents, social secretaries, promoters and other potential musical employers. Ford, the employment promotion officer at the time of writing, makes the vital point that

> Musicians must be prepared to evaluate and market their performances . . . If only more musicians would think about this aspect, rather than thinking that the world owes them a living just because they are musicians. We live in an age dominated by high technology – video recorders, the compact disc, micro computers, cable and satellite television, and hard sell, where music is a commodity, and is marketed accordingly. Musicians must, more than ever before, be prepared to market themselves or be left behind, remembered only as part of a bygone age. (Ford, 1985)

Whilst the Musicians' Union is able to provide various support systems, its main message is that support for all forms of music should continue to be the responsibility of the community through state and local government funding, and it has campaigned vigorously against the break up of vital support systems such as the Greater London Council (GLC) and the metropolitan counties. Relating to this, an organization was formed in 1983 named the National Campaign for the Arts, with an emphasis on research and the provision of information to press, politicians and public. Lobbying concentrates on the arts as a whole, to the long-term benefit of everyone, rather than on individual arts organizations. Crine (1986), director of the campaign, states that

> We aim to persuade the public and politicians that the arts are important and that a positive and well constructed policy for the arts is a must for *all*

parties. The problem we have to combat is greater than the attitudes of any one government to expenditure on arts services: the arts in this country suffer from long-term under-funding and from a lack of recognition of the contribution they make to the rest of society. Britain spends less on the arts per head of population than any comparable country such as France, Italy, West Germany or Austria. This is unjustifiable and absurd for a country which numbers the arts amongst its greatest assets.

The above comments are highly relevant to the lot of the popular musician.

On a slightly more optimistic note, with regard to the promotion of jazz, Cumming (1984) states that during recent years the regional jazz organizations and touring circuits have expanded, with a boost from the Arts Council of Great Britain and the Regional Arts Authorities. At the present time there are five regionally based administrations. The Arts Council also funds a national touring body named Jazz Services with an additional brief for education and information linked with the regional organizations. Nevertheless, Cumming (1984) feels that jazz, in all its forms, is still chronically under-funded in relation to other art forms.

One extremely bleak aspect of the promotion of popular music is recorded in an Insight article in the *Sunday Times* (1986). In 1968 an ambitious project to build a national jazz centre in London was launched with the backing of eminent jazz enthusiasts and financial support from the GLC, the English Tourist Board, the Arts Council, the Musicians' Union and many private donations. At the time of writing, the building, originally intended to be opened in 1981, is still only two-thirds finished. Debts of £750,000 have been incurred, and a further £1.6 million is needed to complete it. This is a glaring indictment of the gross mismanagement of the project, and points to an urgent need for competent management in certain areas of the promotion of jazz and other forms of popular music.

In conclusion, worthy bodies such as the Musicians' Union are doing much to further the cause of the popular musician, but there is still more yet to be done.

The present state of popular music education

Turning to music education, promising developments have taken place in recent years, and continue to take place, even though, as yet, the situation is far from ideal.

Salaman (1985) discusses the effect that the new GCSE sixteen plus examinations will have on the course of music education. In the past, GCE 'O' level music courses have tended to follow a formal, 'classical' approach, with an emphasis on teaching about music rather than teaching music itself. The basic content of 'O' level music courses has been harmony and counterpoint, set works, history of music and aural training. With the introduction of the GCSE, there will be a much greater emphasis upon living musical activity in the classroom. This in turn will lead to changes in 'A' level, university and college music courses, so that they relate more closely to the requirements of 'real' musicians, with an accent on original composition and improvisation of various kinds, including jazz. This is indeed a hopeful development.

Hosier (1985) states that in the past five years there have been new attitudes and developments in music colleges, with a move to make courses much more relevant to the demands of performers in training. Teaching will prepare the musician for a far wider variety of playing situations, including recording studio work and TV commercials. A number of music colleges are now introducing jazz and rock courses. In 1982, the Guildhall School of Music in London started a postgraduate jazz and rock course, to prepare advanced students for commercial work and at the same time to create in the School a reservoir of jazz experience that would satisfy the needs of any student who enjoyed playing jazz. The big band has a nucleus of jazz course players, but is open to all performers who pass an audition. The jazz course has brought musicians into the school who can teach jazz improvisation, and many so-called 'straight' players are finding that jazz develops new aural awareness and frees them from dependence on notation.

Big bands are also part of the curriculum at the Trinity College of Music, London, and the Royal Northern College of Music, Manchester, while Salford College of Technology now offers a two-year Diploma in Popular Music with Recording. The City University, London, offers a B.Sc. in Music which includes the study of jazz and popular music and the National Centre for Orchestral Studies, Goldsmiths' College, London, has courses which aim to prepare students to deal with, among other things, session music. The City of Leeds College of Music instituted the first jazz and light music course in Britain in 1968, and this remains the only British College to provide a full-time degree-equivalent course in popular music.

Many local education authorities now have youth and rehearsal jazz orchestras and rock and pop ensembles, as part of evening and weekend courses. Education authorities that provide these include Barnsley, Calderdale, Doncaster, Dudley, Huddersfield and Manchester.

In 1983, The Arts Council set up an experimental scheme entitled

Jazz in Education, in collaboration with the regional arts associations and the Musicians' Union, with advice and support from the British Association of Jazz Education. It aims to develop and improve the knowledge, understanding and practice of jazz, to make it accessible to a wider audience and to stimulate awareness of the contribution of jazz to music education. The intention is that an increasing number of pilot projects will take place, involving musicians and educators. Funds for each project will come from the Arts Council, the Musicians' Union, the regional arts associations and local education authorities.

A further development in popular music education has been the rock workshops which have been organized regularly by the Musicians' Union since 1976. A band of experienced rock musicians tour the country giving concerts, demonstrations and lectures in popular music techniques.

The situation in popular music education can therefore be described as promising, but to be realistic the fact must be faced that at the present time popular music plays only a small part on the curriculum of most schools and colleges. In America, on the other hand, as Cook (1986) states, virtually every college and university has a jazz orchestra and other popular music ensembles. There, Cook suggests: 'With its network of college orchestras, mainstream modern jazz is a vocabulary which can be learned inside out. Ever more youthful virtuosos come out of those huge ranks.'

Conclusions

The authors feel that it is largely through a new, enlightened attitude of governments to the arts and a change in popular music education that the lot of the popular musician will be improved, with a consequent lessening of stress in his life and career. Change has been initiated, but it demands even greater impetus. Music educators should generally become aware, and put across to children and their parents the fact that popular music can be a worthwhile, viable and respectable career, as much or more so than other careers in the present economic climate, rather than just a poor alternative to a 'real' job.

The following three factors are of prime importance:

1 Every music college should run a popular music course in parallel with, and of equal standing to, classical music courses. Perhaps a similar approach could be adopted to that of art colleges, where art students can specialize either in fine art or graphic design.
2 Incorporated with every popular music course should be a stress

management course which teaches various relaxation strategies and cognitive coping techniques.

3 Also incorporated into every popular music course should be a course concerned with the business side of popular music, dealing with the problems of contracts, royalties, and management relationships.

Thus will the student be more properly prepared for a career in popular music. The groundwork has been laid, but the main changes are yet to come.

Summary of the results of the survey

Popular musicians overall perceived themselves to be highly stressed. Their main worry was that they would not be able to play to the best of their ability, and the highest stresses related to the variety of problems which might stop them from doing this, for instance, instruments not working properly, inadequate rehearsals, fatigue and so forth. The number one pressure was 'feeling that you must reach or maintain the standards of musicianship that you set for yourself', and the main predictors of ill health were performance and performance-related anxiety, and poor work conditions.

Popular musicians emerged as 'driven' individuals, striving towards artistic self-satisfaction and a high level of performance. Although they exhibited a good level of general health, and did not appear to smoke cigarettes, drink alcohol or use illegal drugs excessively compared to general population norms, they suffered from above-average levels of anxiety, and were frequently dissatisfied with specific gigs that they had to play, while enjoying their work as musicians overall. The most popular way of coping with stress was to use humour.

Jazz musicians suffered more than other musicians from performance anxiety and the ignorance of the public, but also experienced the highest level of enjoyment in their work. They used coping methods such as yoga and relaxation exercises more than other musicians. Pop musicians were concerned to a far greater extent than others regarding their involvement in the pop music industry, and their need for commercial success. The highest stress for pop musicians was 'coming into conflict with recording, management or agency executives who are involved in your career and who do not share your musical ideals'. They were also more prone to certain health problems which manifested themselves as feelings of immobilization or inertia, and they used more frequently than other musicians the drugs cannabis, amphetamines and cocaine.

Commercial session musicians emerged as being the most secure and least stressed of all the groups of popular musicians. They were the highest paid, with 46 per cent of them earning over £20,000 per annum, and were older and more often married, with more children. They were also the least frequent cigarette smokers, but the heaviest drinkers.

On the other hand, commercial freelance musicians were the most highly stressed group. They had the poorest overall health, and were the highest percentage to say that they did not find real enjoyment in their work as musicians.

In looking at individual instrumentalists, guitarists and trumpeters emerged with distinctive profiles. Guitarists had the most anxious personalities, while trumpeters had the lowest degree of anxiety, had the fewest problems playing their instruments, and used more often than other instrumentalists such positive coping strategies as meditation techniques.

A small number of female popular musicians filled in questionnaires, and these were compared to their male counterparts. Female musicians were overall less well-paid than males, and also exhibited less confidence in their ability in playing situations.

Response to the survey was good, and musicians seemed to feel that it was worthwhile carrying out a project of this nature. The results showed that popular musicians are carrying out a hard, worthwhile job, and that they do suffer from the effects of stress. It appears that popular musicians still tend to be treated as second-class citizens when compared to their classical colleagues, who already have the International Society for the Study of Tension in Performance. Since, from the results of our survey, performance anxiety is one of the main predictors of ill health in popular musicians, they too are entitled to some training in anxiety-management techniques. Every music college should run a popular music course, which would include training in stress management and also training in how to deal with the pop music business.

Appendix
Musician's questionnaire

Section A

For purposes of statistical analysis ONLY, please answer the following questions about yourself. Your answers will remain ANONYMOUS AND STRICTLY CONFIDENTIAL. However, your information is CRUCIAL to the study.

What is the main instrument you play? ....

What other instruments do you play? ....

Do you play any of these types of music? Please CIRCLE the most appropriate response.

	Never	Rarely	Sometimes	Often	Mainly
1 Jazz	1	2	3	4	5
2 Rock (heavy rock, 'adult oriented', new wave, etc.)	1	2	3	4	5
3 Pop music	1	2	3	4	5
4 Commercial/easy listening/ middle-of-the-road-music	1	2	3	4	5
5 Dance band music (i.e. quick steps etc.)	1	2	3	4	5
6 Jazz-funk/fusion/crossover music	1	2	3	4	5
7 Disco funk	1	2	3	4	5
8 Reggae	1	2	3	4	5
9 Soul/rhythm and blues	1	2	3	4	5
10 Folk	1	2	3	4	5
11 Other (please state)	1	2	3	4	5

	Never	Rarely	Sometimes	Often	Mainly
How often do you work, AS A MEMBER OF A GIGGING BAND?	1	2	3	4	5
How often do you work, AS A RESIDENT MUSICIAN? (e.g. in nightclub band, ballroom, theatre orchestra etc.)	1	2	3	4	5
How often do you work AS A SESSION MUSICIAN? (e.g. in recording, radio, TV studios)	1	2	3	4	5

Section B

Could you please circle the number that best reflects the degree to which the particular statement is a SOURCE OF PRESSURE IN YOUR LIFE AND WORK AS A MUSICIAN.

Only when a statement/situation does not apply to you, circle NA for *Not Applicable*, e.g. circle NA for '*doing a long tour*' if you never do long tours.

Definitions
Pressure is defined as A PROBLEM, SOMETHING YOU FIND DIFFICULT TO COPE WITH, ABOUT WHICH YOU FEEL WORRIED OR ANXIOUS.

Codes: 5 = a source of EXTREME pressure.
3 = a source of MODERATE pressure.
1 = NO PRESSURE at all.

	No pressure at all				A great deal of pressure	
1 Playing at a venue with bad conditions, e.g. poor dressing rooms, poor acoustics, small stage	1	2	3	4	5	NA
2 Working in the enclosed and isolated environment of the recording studio	1	2	3	4	5	NA
3 Working at night, often into the early hours	1	2	3	4	5	NA
4 Doing a long tour	1	2	3	4	5	NA
5 Doing recording sessions or rehearsals during the day, then having to do a gig at night	1	2	3	4	5	NA
6 Having to read and play a difficult part at a recording session or gig	1	2	3	4	5	NA
7 Playing where there is inadequate rehearsal or preparation	1	2	3	4	5	NA
8 Having to play after travelling a long distance	1	2	3	4	5	NA
9 Having to work when work is available, making it difficult to take holidays	1	2	3	4	5	NA
10 Working alone, composing or arranging	1	2	3	4	5	NA
11 Feeling lonely or bored in strange towns or hotels when on tour	1	2	3	4	5	NA

		No pressure at all				A great deal of pressure	
12	Having to do a routine, repetitive gig such as working in a theatre pit orchestra	1	2	3	4	5	NA
13	Waiting around for long periods at the gig before it's time to play	1	2	3	4	5	NA
14	Effects of noise when the music is heavily amplified	1	2	3	4	5	NA
15	Endangering your life by having to drive a long distance after a gig when you're tired	1	2	3	4	5	NA
16	The expensiveness of instruments and other musical equipment	1	2	3	4	5	NA
17	Instruments or equipment not working properly	1	2	3	4	5	NA
18	Coping with an instrument that is physically difficult to play	1	2	3	4	5	NA
19	Keeping up with new equipment and technology	1	2	3	4	5	NA
20	Having to play music you don't like, in order to earn a living	1	2	3	4	5	NA
21	Worrying because of the lack of gigs	1	2	3	4	5	NA
22	Feeling that you need to become better known and/or better paid	1	2	3	4	5	NA
23	Worrying about being sacked from a gig or band	1	2	3	4	5	NA
24	Worrying about the lack of pensions and benefits in the music profession	1	2	3	4	5	NA
25	Waiting for payment to come through from a gig or session	1	2	3	4	5	NA
26	Finding it difficult to get a good recording or management deal for your band or musical project	1	2	3	4	5	NA
27	If you are a member of a famous band, feeling that this puts special pressures on you	1	2	3	4	5	NA
28	Feeling that you have reached the top too soon	1	2	3	4	5	NA

		No pressure at all				A great deal of pressure	
29	Personality clashes with, or jealousy of other musicians	1	2	3	4	5	NA
30	Coping with criticisms in the music press or from other musicians	1	2	3	4	5	NA
31	Having to mingle socially with other musicians so that you will keep getting gigs	1	2	3	4	5	NA
32	Feeling that if you are too intense or honest about your music, other musicians will regard you with suspicion	1	2	3	4	5	NA
33	Coping with a bandleader or musical director whose musical ideas clash with yours	1	2	3	4	5	NA
34	Having to sack a musician if you are a bandleader	1	2	3	4	5	NA
35	In the recording studio, disagreeing with your producer or engineer	1	2	3	4	5	NA
36	Getting musicians to deputize at short notice	1	2	3	4	5	NA
37	Worrying about all the musicians getting to the gig on time	1	2	3	4	5	NA
38	Feeling that playing is only one part of being a musician, e.g. also having to drive the band's transport, set up equipment, repair faulty amps., hustle for gigs etc.	1	2	3	4	5	NA
39	As an artist, coming into conflict with recording, management or agency executives who are involved in your career and who do not share your musical ideals	1	2	3	4	5	NA
40	Feeling that decisions about your band's musical policy are taken without consulting you	1	2	3	4	5	NA
41	Feeling alienated from people who lead a 'normal, everyday' lifestyle and who may regard you as a 'second-class citizen'	1	2	3	4	5	NA

	No pressure at all			A great deal of pressure		
42 Stress put upon personal relationships, e.g. marriage, due to unusual working hours and long periods away from home	1	2	3	4	5	NA
43 Feeling 'high' after a gig and having to unwind, often with the use of alcohol or drugs	1	2	3	4	5	NA
44 Feeling tense or nervous when playing a live gig *with your regular band*	1	2	3	4	5	NA
45 Feeling tense or nervous when playing a live gig *as a session musician*	1	2	3	4	5	NA
46 Feeling tense or nervous when playing in the recording studio *with your regular band*	1	2	3	4	5	NA
47 Feeling tense or nervous when playing in the recording studio *as a session musician*	1	2	3	4	5	NA
48 Doing an audition	1	2	3	4	5	NA
49 Feeling that you must reach or maintain the standards of musicianship that you set for yourself	1	2	3	4	5	NA
50 Worrying that your ability to play will leave you	1	2	3	4	5	NA
51 Feeling that your musical ability is not appreciated because of the public's ignorance about music	1	2	3	4	5	NA
52 Worrying that your style of playing is no longer fashionable	1	2	3	4	5	NA
53 Worrying about the prospect of flying when you have a tour or gig in a foreign country	1	2	3	4	5	NA
54 Other (please state)	1	2	3	4	5	NA

....

....

Section C

Please answer the following questions by CIRCLING the most appropriate response unless otherwise instructed. Your answers will remain ANONYMOUS AND STRICTLY CONFIDENTIAL.

1 What is your age?

Under 20	1
20–29	2
30–39	3
40–49	4
50–59	5
60–69	6

2 Are you:

Single	1
Married	2
Separated	3
Divorced	4
Widowed	5

3 Number of children:

None	1
One	2
Two	3
Three	4
Four or more	5

4 What is the highest educational qualification, if any, you have attained?

None	1
GCE 'O' Level/CSE	2
'A' Level/Ordinary National Diploma	3
Higher National Diploma	4
Music degree or diploma	5
Other university degree	6
M.A./M.Sc.	7
Ph.D.	8

5 Did you work in a non musical-job on leaving school?

Yes 1 Please specify ....

No 2 ....

6 At what age did you become a professional musician?

....

7 What is your annual salary?

Under £4,000	1
£4,000–£6,000	2
£6,000–£8,000	3
£8,000–£10,000	4
£10,000–£12,000	5
£12,000–£14,000	6
£14,000–£16,000	7
£16,000–£18,000	8
£18,000–£20,000	9
Over £20,000	10

8 Do you teach as well as play?

Yes	1
No	2

Section D

Below is a list of different troubles and complaints which people often have. Please circle the number which best reflects how often you have felt like this during the last *three months*.

I feel like this:

		Never	Rarely	Sometimes	Often	Always
1	Do you ever have any trouble getting to sleep or staying asleep?	1	2	3	4	5
2	Have you ever been bothered by nervousness, feeling fidgety or tense?	1	2	3	4	5
3	Are you ever troubled by headaches or pains in the head?	1	2	3	4	5
4	Are there any times when you just don't feel like eating?	1	2	3	4	5
5	Are there times when you get tired very easily?	1	2	3	4	5
6	How often are you bothered by having an upset stomach?	1	2	3	4	5
7	Do you find it difficult to get up in the morning?	1	2	3	4	5
8	Does ill health ever affect the amount of work you do?	1	2	3	4	5
9	Are you ever bothered by shortness of breath when you are not exercising or working hard?	1	2	3	4	5
10	Do you ever feel 'put out' if something unexpected happens?	1	2	3	4	5
11	Are there times when you tend to cry easily?	1	2	3	4	5
12	Have you ever been bothered by your heart beating hard?	1	2	3	4	5
13	Do you ever smoke, drink, or eat more than you should?	1	2	3	4	5
14	Do you ever have spells of dizziness?	1	2	3	4	5
15	Are you ever bothered by nightmares?	1	2	3	4	5
16	Do your muscles ever tremble enough to bother you (e.g. hands tremble, eyes twitch)?	1	2	3	4	5
17	Do you ever feel mentally exhausted and have difficulty in concentrating or thinking clearly?	1	2	3	4	5
18	Are you troubled by your hands sweating so that you feel damp and clammy?	1	2	3	4	5
19	Have there ever been times when you couldn't take care of things because you just couldn't get going?	1	2	3	4	5
20	Do you ever just want to be left alone?	1	2	3	4	5

TO THE REMAINING QUESTIONS PLEASE ANSWER 'YES' OR 'NO'.

	NO	YES
21 Do you feel you are bothered by all sorts of pains and ailments in different parts of your body?	1	2
22 For the most part, do you feel healthy enough to carry out the things you would like to do?	1	2
23 Have you ever felt that you were going to have a nervous breakdown?	1	2
24 Have you any particular physical or health problem?	1	2

Section E

I   How often do you use the following measures to relax?

	Never	Rarely	Sometimes	Often	Always
1 Take aspirin	1	2	3	4	5
2 Take tranquillisers or other medication	1	2	3	4	5
3 Drink coffee, coke, or eat frequently	1	2	3	4	5
4 Smoke cigarettes	1	2	3	4	5
5 Have an alcoholic drink	1	2	3	4	5
6 Smoke cannabis	1	2	3	4	5
7 Use relaxation techniques (meditation, yoga)	1	2	3	4	5
8 Use informal relaxation techniques (e.g. take time out for deep breathing, imagining pleasant scenes)	1	2	3	4	5
9 Exercise	1	2	3	4	5
10 Talk to someone you know	1	2	3	4	5
11 Leave your work area and go somewhere (time out, sick days etc.)	1	2	3	4	5
12 Use humour	1	2	3	4	5
13 Other	1	2	3	4	5

....

II   Over the past year, which of the following best describes your typical drinking habits? (One drink is a single whisky, gin or brandy; a glass of wine, sherry or port; or HALF A PINT of beer.)

Teetotal	1
An occasional drink	2
Several drinks a week, but not every day	3
Regularly, 1 or 2 drinks a day	4
Regularly, 3–6 drinks a day	5
Regularly, more than 6 drinks a day	6

III   Re: cigarette smoking. Which of the following statements is most nearly true for you?

I have never smoked regularly	1
I have given up smoking	2
I am currently smoking	3

IV   If you are currently smoking, please circle the number which constitutes your daily average consumption

0–5 a day	1
5–10 a day	2
10–15 a day	3
15–20 a day	4
20–30 a day	5
30–40 a day	6
40 plus a day	7

V   How often, if ever, do you use the following drugs? Your answers will remain ANONYMOUS AND STRICTLY CONFIDENTIAL, and are for STATISTICAL ANALYSIS only.

	Never	Rarely	Sometimes	Often	A lot
Cannabis	1	2	3	4	5
LSD	1	2	3	4	5
Amphetamines	1	2	3	4	5
Cocaine	1	2	3	4	5
Heroin	1	2	3	4	5

VI   Please circle the number which best describes how you feel about your work at the present time.

	Strongly Agree	Agree	Undecided	Disagree	Strongly Disagree
I feel fairly well satisfied with my present gig(s)	1	2	3	4	5
I find real enjoyment in my work as a musician	1	2	3	4	5

VII   Could you please circle the ONE number which you feel most closely represents your own behaviour, e.g. for item 1, 'Never late v. casual about appointments', if you tend to be casual about appointments, as opposed to never being late, you might circle number 8.

1	Never late	1 2 3 4 5 6 7 8 9 10 11	Casual about appointments
2	Competitive	1 2 3 4 5 6 7 8 9 10 11	Not competitive

3	Anticipates what others are going to say (nods, interrupts, finishes for them)	1 2 3 4 5 6 7 8 9 10 11 Good listener
4	Always rushed	1 2 3 4 5 6 7 8 9 10 11 Never feels rushed (even under pressure)
5	Impatient whilst waiting	1 2 3 4 5 6 7 8 9 10 11 Can wait patiently
6	Goes all out	1 2 3 4 5 6 7 8 9 10 11 Casual
7	Tries to do many things at once, thinks what he is about to do next	1 2 3 4 5 6 7 8 9 10 11 Takes things one at a time
8	Emphatic in speech	1 2 3 4 5 6 7 8 9 10 11 Slow, deliberate talker
9	Wants good job recognized by others	1 2 3 4 5 6 7 8 9 10 11 Cares about satisfying himself no matter what others think
10	Fast (eating, working, etc.)	1 2 3 4 5 6 7 8 9 10 11 Slow doing things
11	Hard driving	1 2 3 4 5 6 7 8 9 10 11 Easy going
12	Hides feelings	1 2 3 4 5 6 7 8 9 10 11 Expresses feelings
13	Few interests outside work	1 2 3 4 5 6 7 8 9 10 11 Many outside interests
14	Ambitious	1 2 3 4 5 6 7 8 9 10 11 Unambitious

Section F

Thank you for completing this questionnaire. Please write below any other comments you may wish to add, e.g. other stressful factors in your life and work not mentioned in the questionnaire.

References

Abelin, T., Reymond, M.C. and Grandjean, E. (1962) 'Untersuchungen über die berufliche Beanspruchung von Orchestermusikern', *Zeitschrift Präventivmedizin*, 7: 267–83.

Amstell, Billy (1986) *Don't fuss, Mr Ambrose*. Tunbridge Wells: Spellmount.

Baker, T. (1984) Letter, *The Musician* (Journal of the Musicians' Union), December.

Barnes, Richard (1982) *The Who: Maximum R & B*. London: Eel Pie Publishing.

Bayer, L.J. (1982) 'The Stress Process in Professional Musicians: An Exploratory Study.' Unpublished Ph.D. Thesis, University of Cincinnati.

Becker, H.S. (1963) *Outsiders: Studies in the Sociology of Deviance*. New York: Free Press.

Ben-Or, N. (1983) 'The Alexander Technique – its Relevance to Performance', *Journal of the International Society for the Study of Tension in Performance*, 1 (1): 39–42.

Black, J. (1984a) 'Boring but Important Bits', pp. 69–82 in International Association of Fan Clubs (eds), *Inside Pop Music*. Kingston-upon-Thames: C.H.W. Roles & Associates.

Black, J. (1984b) 'Coping as a Megastar', pp. 185–203 in International Association of Fan Clubs (eds), *Inside Pop Music*. Kingston-upon-Thames: C.H.W. Roles & Associates.

Bortner, R.W. and Rosenman, R.H (1967) 'The Measurement of Pattern A Behaviour', *Journal of Chronic Disease*, 20: 525–33.

Brantigan, C.O. (1984) 'Stage Fright: Characteristics, Physiology and the Role of Beta-sympathetic Receptors in its Modification', *Journal of the International Society for the Study of Tension in Performance*, 1 (2): 13–20.

Brantigan, C.O. and Brantigan, T.A. (1982) 'Effect of Beta Blockade and Beta Stimulation on Stage Fright', *American Journal of Medicine*, 72 (1): 88–94.

British Institute of Management (1974) 'The Management Threshold', BIM Paper OPN, 11.

Brown, Mick (1987) 'Poor Boy, Rich Boy George', *Sunday Times Magazine*, 12 April.

Burman, M.A., Pennebaker, J.W. and Glass, D.C. (1975) 'Time Consciousness, Achievement Striving and the Type 'A', Coronary-Prone Behaviour Pattern', *Journal of Abnormal Psychology*, 84: 76–9.

Caplan, R.D., Cobb, S., and French, J.R.P. (1975) 'Job Demands and Workers' Health', US Department of Health, Education and Welfare Publication.

Caplan, R.D., Cobb, S. and French, J.R.P. (1976) 'Relationships of Cessation of Smoking with Job Stress, Personality and Social Support', *Journal of Applied Psychology*, 60: 211–19.

Carruthers, M. (1969) 'Aggression and Atheroma', *Lancet*, 6 December, 1170.

Carruthers, M. (1980) 'Hazardous Occupations and the Heart', pp. 3–22 in C.L. Cooper and R. Payne (eds), *Current Concerns in Occupational Stress*. Chichester: Wiley.

Cattell, R.B. and Butcher, H.J. (1968) *The Prediction of Achievement and Creativity*. New York: Bobbs-Merrill.

Cobb, S. and Rose, R.M. (1973) 'Hypertension, Peptic Ulcer, and Diabetes in Air Traffic Controllers', *Journal of the Australian Medical Association*, 224: 489–92.

Colquhoun, W.P. (1970) 'Circadian Rhythms, Mental Efficiency, and Shift Work', pp. 28–30 in P.R. Davis (ed.), *Proceedings of the Symposium in Performance under Sub-Optimal Conditions*. London: Taylor & Francis.

Cook, R. (1986) 'Spotlight on the Young Ones', *Sunday Times*, 19 October.

Cooper, C.L. (1980a) 'Coronaries: the Risk to Working Women', *The Times*, 8 December.

Cooper, C.L. (1980b) 'Work Stress in White and Blue Collar Jobs', *Bulletin of the British Psychological Society*, 33: 49–51.

Cooper, C.L. (1980c) 'Dentists under Pressure: A Social Psychological Study', pp. 3–17 in C.L. Cooper and J. Marshall (eds), *White Collar and Professional Stress*. London: Wiley.

Cooper, C.L. (1983) *Stress Research: Issues for the Eighties*. Chichester: Wiley.

Cooper, C.L. and Davidson, M.J. (1982) *High Pressure: Working Lives of Women Managers*. Glasgow: Fontana.

Cooper, C.L. and Marshall, J. (1976) 'Occupational Sources of Stress: A Review of the Literature Relating to Coronary Heart Disease and Mental Ill Health', *Journal of Occupational Psychology*, 49: 11–28.

Cooper, C.L. and Marshall, J. (1978) *Understanding Executive Stress*. London: Macmillan.

Cooper, C.L. and Marshall, J. (1980) *White Collar and Professional Stress*. Chichester: Wiley.

Cooper, C.L. and Melhuish, A. (1980) 'Occupational Stress and Managers', *Journal of Occupational Medicine*, 22: 588–92.

Cooper, C.L. and Roden, J. (1985) 'Mental Health and Satisfaction among Tax Officers', *Social Science and Medicine*, 21 (7): 747–51.

Cooper, C.L. and Smith, M.J. (1985) *Job Stress and Blue Collar Work*. Chichester: Wiley.

Cooper, C.L., Davidson, M.J., and Robinson, P. (1982) 'Stress in the Police Service', *Journal of Occupational Medicine*, 24: 30–6.

Cooper, C.L., Mallinger, M., and Kahn, R. (1978) 'Identifying Sources of Occupational Stress among Dentists', *Journal of Occupational Psychology*, 51: 227–34.

Coryell, J. and Friedman, L. (1978) *Jazz-Rock Fusion*. London: Marion Boyars.

Crine, S. (1986) 'Why We Need a Strong Arts Lobby', *The Musician*, April.

Cross, P., Cattell, R.B. and Butcher, H.J. (1967) 'The Personality Pattern of Creative Artists', *British Journal of Educational Psychology*, 37: 292–9.

Crump, J.H., Cooper, C.L. and Maxwell, V.B. (1981) 'Stress among Air Traffic Controllers: Occupational Sources of Coronary Heart Disease Risk', *Journal of Occupational Behaviour*, 2: 293–303.

Csikszentmihalyi, M. and Getzels, J.L. (1973) 'The Personality of Young Artists: An Empirical and Theoretical Exploration', *British Journal of Psychology*, 64 (1): 91–104.

Cumming, J. (1984) 'Jazz is . . .', *The Musician*, April.

Dahl, L. (1984) *Stormy Weather: The Music and Lives of a Century of Jazz Women*. London: Quartet Books.

Davidson, M.J. and Cooper, C.L. (1981) 'A Model of Occupational Stress', *Journal of Occupational Medicine*, 23 (8): 564–74.

Davidson, M.J., and Cooper, C.L. (1983) *Stress and the Woman Manager*. Oxford: Martin Robertson.

Davidson, M.J., and Cooper, C.L. (1984) *Working Woman: An International Survey*. Chichester: Wiley.

Davidson, M.J., and Davidson, H.J. (1980) 'Stress in the Recording Studio', *Recording Engineer/Producer*, 11 (6): 14–16.

Davidson, M.J. and Veno, A. (1980) 'Stress and the Policeman', pp. 131–66 in C.L. Cooper and J. Marshall (eds), *White Collar and Professional Stress*. London: Wiley.

Davies, J.B. (1978) *The Psychology of Music*. London: Hutchinson.

Dearing, J. (1981) 'Are Drums Harming Your Ears?' *Modern Drummer*, 5 (8): 25–8.

Dembroski, T.M. and MacDougall, J.M. (1982) 'Coronary-Prone Behaviour, Social Psychophysiology, and Coronary Heart Disease', pp. 39–62 in J.R. Eiser (ed.), *Social Psychology and Behavioural Medicine*. Chichester: Wiley.

Diamond, J. (1986) 'Frankie Goes to Lubbock Fine', *Sunday Times Magazine*, 12 October.

Doyle, G. (1984) 'The Task of the Violinist: Skill, Stress and the Alexander Technique.' Unpublished Ph.D. Thesis, University of Lancaster.

Duffy, E. (1962) *Activation and Behaviour*. New York: Wiley.

Ehrlich, Cyril (1985) *The Music Profession in Britain since the Eighteenth Century: A Social History*. Oxford: Clarendon Press.

Erickson, J.M., Pugh, W.M. and Gunderson, K.E. (1972) 'Status Congruency as a Prediction of Job Satisfaction and Life Stress', *Journal of Applied Psychology*, 56: 523–5.

Eysenck, H.J. and Eysenck, S.B.G. (1975) *Manual of the Eysenck Personality Questionnaire*. London: Hodder & Stoughton.

Ford, J. (1985) '"Live in '85" Campaign Report', *The Musician*, August.

Frame, Pete (ed.) (1974) *The Road to Rock*. London: Charisma Books.

French, J. and Caplan, R. (1972) 'Organizational Stress and Individual Strain', pp. 31–66 in Marrow, A.J. (ed.), *The Failure of Success*. New York: Amacon.

Friedman, M. and Rosenman, R.H. (1974) *Type A Behaviour and Your Heart*. London: Wildwood House.

Frith, S. (1983) *Sound Effects: Youth, Leisure, and the Politics of Rock*. London: Constable.

Fry, H.J.H. (1985) 'Music Making and Overuse Injuries', *Journal of the International Society for the Study of Tension in Performance*, 1 (3): 41–50.

Garfield, S. (1986) *Expensive Habits: The Dark Side of the Music Industry*. London: Faber & Faber.

General Household Survey (1980) London: HMSO.

Gillman, Peter and Gillman, Leni (1986) *Alias David Bowie*. London: Hodder & Stoughton.

Glass, D.C. (1977) *Behaviour Patterns, Stress and Coronary Disease*. Hillsdale, NJ: Lawrence Erlbaum.

Godbolt, Jim (1984) *A History of Jazz in Britain 1919–1950*. London: Quartet Books.

Gotz, K.O. and Gotz, K. (1979a) 'Personality Characteristics of Professional Artists', *Perceptual and Motor Skills*, 49: 327–34.

Gotz, K.O. and Gotz, K. (1979b) 'Personality Characteristics of Successful Artists', *Perceptual and Motor Skills*, 49: 919–24.

Gurin, G., Veroff, J. and Feld, S. (1960) *Americans View their Mental Health*. New York: Basic Books.

Haider, M. and Groll-Knapp, E. (1981) 'Psychophysiological Investigation into the Stress Experienced by Musicians in a Symphony Orchestra', pp. 15–34 in M. Piparek (ed.), *Stress and Music*. Vienna: Wilhelm Braumuller.

Havas, K. (1973) *Stage Fright: Its Causes and Cures with Special Reference to Violin Playing*. London: Bosworth.

Hentoff, N. (1961) *The Jazz Life*. New York: Dial Press.

Herman, G. (1982) *Rock'n'Roll Babylon*. London: Plexus.

Hit (1985) 'Drugs: The *Hit* Survey', 26 October.

Hochberg, F.H., Leffert, R.D. and Silverman, R.J. (1983) 'Physicians' Views of Physical Problems', *Journal of the International Society for the Study of Tension in Performance*, 1 (1): 23–33.

Hosier, J. (1985) 'Preparing Performers – Developments at the Music Colleges', pp. 9–12 in M. Barton and J. Fowler (eds), *British Music Education Yearbook 1985/6*. London: Rhinegold Publishing.

Hrano, M. (1984) 'After the Demo is Accepted' pp. 83–106 in International Association of Fan Clubs (eds), *Inside Pop Music*. Kingston-upon-Thames: C.H.W. Roles & Associates.

Humphrey, M. (1977) 'Review: Eysenck Personality Questionnaire', *Journal of Medical Psychology*, 50: 203–4.

Hurrell, J.J. and Kroes, W.H. (1975) *Stress Awareness*. Cincinnati, Ohio: National Institute for Occupational Safety and Health.

James, I.M. (1984) 'How Players Show Stress Symptoms', *Classical Music*, 17 November.

James, I.M. and Savage, I.T. (1984) 'Beneficial Effect of Nadolol on Anxiety-Induced Disturbances of Performance in Musicians: A Comparison with Diazepam and Placebo', *American Heart Journal*, 108 (4): 1150–55.

James, I.M., Burgoyne, W. and Savage, I.T. (1983) 'Effect of Pindolol on Stress-Related Disturbances of Musical Performance: Preliminary Communication', *Journal of the Royal Society of Medicine*, 76 (3): 194–6.

James, I.M., Griffith, D.N., Pearson, R.M. and Newbury, P. (1977) 'Effect of Oxprenolol on Stage Fright in Musicians', *Lancet*, 5 November, 952–4.

James, I.M., Pearson, R.M., Griffith, D.N., Newbury, P. and Taylor, S.H. (1978) 'Reducing the Somatic Manifestations of Anxiety by Beta-Blockade – A Study of Stage Fright', *Journal of Psychosomatic Research*, 22: 327–37.

Kasl, S.V. (1973) 'Mental Health and Work Environment: An Examination of the Evidence', *Journal of Occupational Medicine*, 15 (6): 506–15.

Kelly, M., and Cooper, C.L. (1981) 'Stress among Blue-Collar Workers', *Employee Relations*, 3: 6–9.

Kemp, A.E. (1980) 'Personality Differences between the Players of String, Woodwind, Brass and Keyboard Instruments, and Singers.' Paper Delivered at the Eighth International Seminar on Research in Music Education, University of Reading School of Education.

Kemp, A.E. (1981) 'The Personality Structure of the Musician: 1 Identifying a Profile of Traits for the Performer', *Psychology of Music*, 9 (1): 3–14.

Kemp, A.E. (1982) 'The Personality Structure of the Musician: 3 The Significance of Sex Differences', *Psychology of Music*, 10 (1): 48–58.

Kendrick, M.J., Craig, K.D., Lawson, D.M. and Davidson, P.D. (1982) 'Cognitive and Behavioural Therapy for Musical-Performance Anxiety', *Journal of Consulting and Clinical Psychology*, 50 (3): 352–62.

Koestler, A. (1969) *The Act of Creation*. London: Hutchinson.

Kroes, W.H. (1976) *Society's Victim – the Policeman – An Analysis of Job Stress in Policing*. New York: Charles C. Thomas.

Kyriacou, C. (1980) 'Sources of Stress among British Teachers: The Contribution of Job Factors and Personality Factors', pp. 113–28 in C.L. Cooper and J. Marshall (eds), *White Collar and Professional Stress*. London: Wiley.

Lancet (1985) 'Editorial: The Music Clinic', 8 June, 1,309–10.

Lehrer, P.M. (1982) 'A Psychologist's Perspective', pp. 134–52 in C. Grindea (ed.), *Tensions in the Performance of Music*. London: Kahn & Averill.

Maccoby, E.E. (ed.) (1966) *The Development of Sex Differences*. London: Tavistock.

Mackinnon, D.W. (1962) 'The Nature and Nurture of Creative Talent', *American Psychologist*, 17 (7): 484–94.

McMichael, A.J. (1978) 'Personality, Behavioural and Situational Modifiers of Work Stressors', pp. 127–47 in C.L. Cooper and R. Payne (eds), *Stress at Work*. Chichester: Wiley.

Margolis, B.L. (1973) 'Stress is a Work Hazard Too', *Industrial Medicine, Occupational Health and Surgery*, 42 (Oct.): 20–3.

Margolis, B., Kroes, W. and Quinn, R. (1974) 'Job Stress: An Unlisted Occupational Hazard', *Journal of Occupational Medicine*, 1 (16): 654–61.

Marshall, J. (1977) 'Job Pressures and Satisfactions at Managerial Levels.' Unpublished Ph.D. Thesis, University of Manchester.

Marshall, J., and Cooper, C.L. (1979) *Executives under Pressure*. London: Macmillan.

Martin, G. (1983) 'Record Production', pp. 266–77 in G. Martin (ed.), *Making Music*. London: Pan Books.

Matthews, K.A. (1982) 'Psychological Perspectives on the Type 'A' Behaviour Pattern', *Psychological Bulletin*, 91 (2): 293–323.

Maxwell, A.E. (1970) *Basic Statistics in Behavioural Research*. Harmondsworth: Penguin.

Monk, T. and Tepas, D. (1985) 'Shift Work', pp. 65–84 in C.L. Cooper and M.J. Smith (eds), *Job Stress and Blue Collar Work*. Chichester: Wiley.

Morton, J. (1986) *Musicians' Union Diary*. London: Musicians' Union.

Neftel, K.A., Adler, R.H., Kappeli, L., Rossi, M., Dolder, M., Kaser, H.E., Bruggesser, H.H. and Vorkauf, H. (1982) 'Stage Fright in Musicians: A Model Illustrating the Effect of Beta Blockers', *Psychosomatic Medicine*, 44 (5): 461–69.

Norman, Philip (1981) *Shout! The True Story of the Beatles*. London: Hamish Hamilton.

Norman, Philip (1984) *The Stones*. London: Elm Tree Books/Hamish Hamilton.

Otway, H.J., and Misenta, R. (1980) 'The Determinants of Operator Preparedness for Emergency Situations in Nuclear Power Plants.' Paper presented at Workshop on Procedural and Organizational Measures for Accident Management, Nuclear Reactors International Institute for Applied Systems Analysis, Laxenburg, Austria.

Pahl, J.M., and Pahl, R.E. (1971) *Managers and their Wives*. London: Allen Lane.

Patterson, M. (1986) *Hooked? NET: The New Approach to Drug Cure*. London: Faber & Faber.

Piparek, M. (1981) 'Psychological Stress and Strain Factors in the Work of a Symphony Orchestra Musician', pp. 3–14 in M. Piparek (ed.), *Stress and Music*. Vienna: Wilhelm Braumuller.

Polon, M. (1979) 'dBs Can be Hazardous to your Health', *Recording Engineer/ Producer*, October: 126–39.

Raeburn, S.D. (1984) 'Occupational Stress and Coping in Professional Rock Musicians.' Unpublished Ph.D. Thesis, The Wright Institute, Berkeley.

Rafky, D. (1974) 'My Husband the Cop', *Police Chief*, 41 (Aug.): 63–5.

Rollins, B.C. and Cannon, K.L. (1974) 'Marital Satisfaction over the Family Life-Cycle: A Re-evaluation', *Journal of Marriage and the Family*, 36 (May): 271–83.

Rollins, B.C. and Feldman, H. (1970) 'Marital Satisfaction over the Family Life Cycle', *Journal of Marriage and the Family*, 32 (Feb.): 20–28.

Rosenman, R.H., Friedman, M. and Straus, R. (1964) 'A Predictive Study of CHD', *Journal of the American Medical Association*, 189: 15–22.

Russek, H.I. and Zohman, B.L. (1958) 'Relative Significance of Hereditary, Diet and Occupational Stress in CHD of Young Adults', *American Journal of Medical Science*, 235: 266–75.

Ryniker, D.H. (1981) 'Dealing with the Aches and Pains of Drumming', *Modern Drummer*, 5 (5): 29–30.

Salaman, W. (1985) 'School Music – A New Approach', pp. 3–7 in M. Barton and J. Fowler (eds), *British Music Education Yearbook 1985/86*. London: Rhinegold Publishing.

Samama, A. (1985) 'Stress and Musicians', *Journal of the International Society for the Study of Tension in Performance*, 3 (3): 33–40.

Schuler, R.S. (1980) 'Definition and Conceptualization of Stress in Organizations', *Organizational Behaviour and Human Performance*, 25: 184–215.

Schulz, W. (1981) 'Analysis of a Symphony Orchestra: Sociological and Socio-Psychological Aspects', pp. 35–56 in M. Piparek (ed.), *Stress and Music*. Vienna: Wilhelm Braumuller.

Selye, H. (1976) *Stress in Health and Disease*. Boston: Butterworths.

Shearlaw, J. (1984) 'On the Road Again', pp. 27–42 in International Association of Fan Clubs (eds), *Inside Pop Music*. Kingston-upon-Thames: C.H.W. Roles & Associates.

Siegel, R.H. (1983) 'Lower Back Problems – And How to Avoid Them', *Modern Drummer*, 7 (8): 22–5.

Social Trends (1983) London: HMSO.

Social Trends (1986) London: HMSO.

Sounds (1979) 'The Grim Reaper's Greatest Hits', 28 April.

Steinmetz, J. (1979) *Conflict/Stress Questionnaire*. San Diego: University of California Medical Center.

Steptoe, A. (1983) 'The Relationship between Tension and the Quality of Musical Performance', *Journal of the International Society for the Study of Tension in Performance*, 1 (1): 12–22.

Steward, S. and Garratt, S. (1984) *Signed, Sealed and Delivered: True Life Stories of Women in Pop*. London: Pluto Press.

Sunday Times (1986) 'Jazz Centre Fiasco could Cost Millions', 1 June.

Tobler, J. and Grundy, S. (1983) *The Guitar Greats*. London: British Broadcasting Corporation.

Trethowan, W.H. (1977) 'Music and Mental Disorder', pp. 399–429 in M. Critchley and R.A. Henson (eds), *Music and the Brain*. London: Heinemann.

Tyler, L. (1965) *The Psychology of Human Differences*. New York: Appleton-Century-Crofts.

Welch, Chris (1984) *Led Zeppelin: The Book*. London: Proteus Books.

Wilson, G.D. (1973) 'Abnormalities of Motivation', pp. 362–89 in H.J. Eysenck (ed.), *Handbook of Abnormal Psychology*. London: Pitman.

Wilson, G.D. (1985) *The Psychology of the Performing Arts*. London: Croom Helm.

Winick, C. (1959) 'The Use of Drugs by Jazz Musicians', *Social Problems*, 7: 240–53.

Wright, C. (1983) 'The Record Industry', pp. 290–7 in G. Martin (ed.), *Making Music*. London: Pan Books.

Index of subjects

Index of popular musicians